Bertolt Brecht

SAINT JOAN OF THE STOCKYARDS

Translated by Frank Jones

EYRE METHUEN · LONDON

COLLABORATORS: H. Borchardt, E. Burri, E. Hauptmann

TRANSLATOR: Frank Jones

Written in 1929-31. First produced at the Deutsches Schaus-
pielhaus, Hamburg, 30 April 1959

CHARACTERS

*Pierpont Mauler, a meat king: Cridle, Lennox, Graham, meat
manufacturers: Slift, a speculator: Joan Dark, lieutenant in the
Black Straw Hats: Martha, soldier in the Black Straw Hats:
Paulus Snyder, major in the Black Straw Hats: Jackson, lieutenant in the Black Straw Hats: Mulberry, a landlord: Mrs
Luckerniddle, a worker's wife: Gloomb, a worker: Mrs Swingurn,
a worker's wife: a waiter: an old man: a broker: an apprentice:
two detectives: five labour leaders: two policemen: and, as groups:
wholesalers, stock-breeders, small speculators, workers, newsboys,
passers-by, journalists, voices, musicians, soldiers, poor folk.*

THE MEAT KING PIERPONT MAULER GETS A LETTER FROM HIS FRIENDS IN NEW YORK

Chicago Stockyards

MAULER, *reading a letter*: 'As we can plainly see, dear Pierpont, the stock market has been badly constipated for some little time. Also tariff walls to the south of us are resisting all our attacks. In view of this it seems advisable, dear Pierpont, to let the packing business go.' I have this hint today from my dear friends in New York. Here comes my partner. *He hides the letter.*

CRIDLE: Well, my dear Pierpont! Why so gloomy?

MAULER:
Remember, Cridle, how some days ago –
We were walking through the stockyards, it was evening –
We stood beside our brand-new packing machine.
Remember, Cridle, the ox that took the blow
Standing there blond, huge, dumbly gazing up
Towards Heaven: I felt the stroke was meant for me.
Oh, Cridle! Oh, our business is bloody.

CRIDLE:
So – the old weakness, Pierpont!
Almost incredible: you, giant of packers
Lord of the stockyards, quaking at the kill
Fainting with pain, all for a fair-haired ox!
Don't tell a soul of this but me, I beg you.

MAULER:
O loyal Cridle!
I oughtn't to have visited the stockyards!
Since I went into this business – that's seven
Years – I'd avoided them; and now – oh, Cridle
I cannot bear it any longer! I'm giving up today.

You take this bloody business, with my share!
I'll let you have it cheap: you above all
For no one else belongs to it like you.

CRIDLE:

How cheap?

MAULER:

No long palaver can be held
On such things by old friends like you and me.
Let's say ten million.

CRIDLE:

That would not be expensive but for Lennox
Who fights with us for every case of meat
And ruins our market with his cut-throat prices
And will break us all if he does not go broke.
Before he falls, and only you can fell him
I shall not take your offer. Until then
Your cunning brain must be in constant practice.

MAULER:

No, Cridle! That poor ox's outcry
Will nevermore go mute within me. Therefore
This Lennox must fall fast, for I myself
Have willed to be a decent man henceforth
And not a butcher. Cridle, come with me
And I will tell you what to do to make
Lennox fall fast. But then you must
Relieve me of this business, which hurts me.

CRIDLE:

If Lennox falls.

Exeunt

2

a

THE COLLAPSE OF THE GREAT PACKING PLANTS

In front of the Lennox Plant

THE WORKERS:

> We are seventy thousand workers in Lennox's packing plant
>   and we
> Cannot live a day longer on such low wages.
> Yesterday our pay was slashed again
> And today the notice is up once more:
> ANYONE NOT SATISFIED
> WITH OUR WAGES CAN GO.
> All right then, let's all go and
> Shit on the wages that get skinnier every day.

A silence.

THE WORKERS:

> For a long time now this work has made us sick
> The factory our hell and nothing
> But cold Chicago's terrors could
> Keep us here. But now
> By twelve hours' work a man can't even
> Earn a stale loaf and
> The cheapest pair of pants. Now
> A man might just as well go off and
> Die like a beast.

A silence.

THE WORKERS:

> What do they take us for? Do they think
> We are going to stand here like steers, ready
> For anything? Are we
> Their chumps? Better lie and rot!
> Let's go right now.

A silence.

THE WORKERS:

It must be six o'clock by now!
Why don't you open up, you sweatshop bosses? Here
Are your steers, you butchers, open up!

They knock.

Maybe they've forgotten us?

Laughter.

THE WORKERS:

Open the gates! We
Want to get into your
Dirt-holes and lousy kitchens
To cook stuffed meat
For the eaters who possess.

A silence.

We demand at least
Our former wages, even though they were too low, at least
A ten-hour day and at least –

A MAN, *crossing the stage*:

What are you waiting for? Don't you know
That Lennox has shut down?

Newsboys run across the stage.

THE NEWSBOYS: Meat king Lennox forced to shut down his
plants! Seventy thousand workers without food or shelter!
M. L. Lennox a victim of bitter competitive struggle with
Pierpont Mauler, well-known meat baron and philanthropist.

THE WORKERS:

Alas!
Hell itself
Shuts its gate in our faces!
We are doomed. Bloody Mauler grips
Our exploiter by the throat and
We are the ones who choke!

b

P. MAULER

A Street

THE NEWSBOYS: Chicago Tribune, noon edition! P. Mauler, meat baron and philanthropist, to attend opening of the P. Mauler Hospitals, largest and most expensive in the world!

P. Mauler passes, with two men.

A PASSER-BY, *to another*: That's P. Mauler. Who are the men walking with him?

THE OTHER: Detectives. They guard him so that he won't be knocked down.

c

TO COMFORT THE MISERY OF THE STOCKYARDS, THE BLACK STRAW HATS LEAVE THEIR MISSION-HOUSE. JOAN'S FIRST DESCENT INTO THE DEPTHS

In front of a Black Straw Hats Mission

JOAN, *at the head of the Black Straw Hat shock troop*:
In gloomy times of bloody confusion
Disorder by order
Planned caprice
Dehumanized humanity
When there is no end to the unrest in our cities:
Into such a world, a world like a slaughter-house –
Summoned by rumours of threatening deeds of violence
To prevent the brute strength of the short-sighted people
From shattering its own tools and
Trampling its own bread-basket to pieces –
We wish to reintroduce
God.
A figure of little glory
Almost of ill repute
No longer admitted

To the sphere of actual life:
But, for the humblest, the one salvation!
Therefore we have decided
To beat the drum for Him
That He may gain a foothold in the regions of misery
And His voice may ring out clearly among the slaughter-
    houses.

To the Black Straw Hats:

And this undertaking of ours is surely
The last of its kind. A last attempt
To set Him upright again in a crumbling world, and that
By means of the lowest.

They march on, drums beating..

d

FROM DAWN TO DARK THE BLACK STRAW HATS WORKED IN
THE STOCKYARDS, BUT WHEN EVENING CAME THEY HAD
ACCOMPLISHED JUST ABOUT NOTHING

In front of the Lennox Plant

A WORKER: They say there's another spell of dirty dealing going
    on at the livestock market. Till it's over we'll have to bide
    our time, I guess, and live on air.
A WORKER: Lights are on in the offices. They're counting up the
    profits.

*The Black Straw Hats arrive. They put up a sign: Room for a
Night, 20 cents; With Coffee, 30 cents; Hot Dogs, 15 cents.*

THE BLACK STRAW HATS, *singing*:
    Attention, your attention!
    We see you, man that's falling
    We hear your cry for help
    We see you, woman calling.
    Halt the autos, stop the traffic!
    Courage, sinking people, we're coming, look our way!

You who are going under
See us, oh, see us, brother, before you say you're beat!
We bring you something to eat
We are still aware
That you are standing out there.
Don't say it can't be helped, for things are changing
The injustice of this world cannot remain
If all the people come and join us marching
And leave their cares behind and help with might and main.
We'll bring up tanks and cannon too
And airplanes there shall be
And battleships over the sea
All to conquer a plate of soup, brother, just for you.
For you, yes, you, poor folk
Are an army vast and grand
So even in times like these
We've all got to lend you a hand!
Forward march! Eyes right! Rifles ready to fire!
Courage, you sinking people, we're coming, look our way!

*During the singing the Black Straw Hats have been distributing
their leaflet, 'The Battle Cry', spoons, plates and soup. The workers
say 'Thank you' and listen to Joan's speech.*

JOAN: We are the Soldiers of the Lord. On account of our hats
we are also called the Black Straw Hats. We march with
drums and flags wherever unrest prevails and acts of violence
threaten, to remind men of the Lord whom they have all
forgotten, and to bring back their souls to Him. We call ourselves soldiers because we are an army and when we are on
the march we have to fight crime and misery, those forces
that want to drag us down. *She begins to ladle out the soup
herself.* That's it, just eat some hot soup and then everything
will look real different, but please give a little thought to Him
who bestows it upon you. And when you think that way you
will see that this is really the complete solution: Strive up-
wards, not downwards. Work for a good position up above,
not here below. Want to be the first man up, not the first man

down. Surely you realize now what sort of trust you can place in the fortunes of this world. None at all. Misfortune comes like the rain, that nobody makes, and still it comes. Tell me, where does all your misfortune come from?

AN EATER: From Lennox & Co.

JOAN: Maybe Mr Lennox has more worries right now than you have. After all, what are you losing? His losses run into millions!

A WORKER: There's not much fat floating in this soup, but it contains plenty of wholesome water and there's no lack of warmth.

ANOTHER WORKER: Shut up, revellers! Listen to the heavenly text, or they'll take away your soup!

JOAN: Quiet! Tell me, dear friends, why are you poor?

A WORKER: Aw, *you* tell *us*.

JOAN: All right, I will tell you: it is not because you aren't blest with worldly goods – that is not for all of us – but because you have no sense of higher things. That is why you are poor. These low pleasures for which you work so hard, a bite to eat, nice homes, the movies, they are just coarse sensual enjoyments, but God's word is a far finer, more inward, more exquisite pleasure. Maybe you can't think of anything sweeter than whipped cream, but God's word, I tell you, is still sweeter, honestly it is, oh, how sweet God's word is! It's like milk and honey, and in it you dwell as in a palace of gold and alabaster. O ye of little faith, the birds of the air have no *Help Wanted* ads and the lilies of the field have no jobs, and yet He feeds them, because they sing His praises. You all want to get to the top, but what kind of top, and how do you propose to get there? And so it's we Straw Hats who ask you, quite practically: What does a man need to rise?

A WORKER: A starched collar.

JOAN: No, not a starched collar. Maybe you need a starched collar to get ahead on earth, but in God's eyes you need much more than that around you, a quite different sort of splendour, but before Him you don't even have a rubber collar on, because you have utterly neglected your entire inner natures.

But how are you going to get to the top – whatever, in your ignorance, you call the top? By brute force? As if force ever caused anything but destruction! You believe that if you rear up on your hind legs there'll be heaven on earth. But I say to you: that way not paradise but chaos is created.

A WORKER *enters running*:
A place was just vacated!
It pays, and it's calling you over
To Plant Number Five!
It looks like a urinal on the outside.
Run!

Three workers put down full plates of soup and run.

JOAN: Hey, you, where are you off to? Talk to you about God, *that* you don't want to hear, eh?

A BLACK STRAW HAT GIRL: The soup's all gone.

THE WORKERS:
The soup's all gone.
Fatless it was and scant
But better than nothing.

All turn away and stand up.

JOAN: Oh, keep your seats, no harm's done, the grand soup of heaven never gives out, you know.

THE WORKERS:
When will you finally
Open your roachy cellars
You butchers of men?

Groups form.

A MAN:
How am I to pay for my little house now, the cute damp thing
With twelve of us in it? Seventeen
Instalments I've paid and now the last is due:
They'll throw us onto the street and never again
Will we see the trampled ground with the yellowish grass
And never breathe again
The accustomed pestilent air.

A SECOND MAN, *in a circle*:
> Here we stand with hands like shovels
> And necks like trucks wanting to sell
> Our hands and necks
> And no one will buy them.

THE WORKERS:
> And our work-tool, a giant pile
> Of steam hammers and cranes
> Barred in behind walls!

JOAN: What's up? Now they're simply leaving! Finished eating, have you? Hope you enjoyed it? Thanks. Why have you listened till now?

A WORKER: For the soup.

JOAN: We'll continue. Sing!

THE BLACK STRAW HATS, *singing*:
> Go straight to the thick of the fight
> Where there's the toughest work to do.
> Sing with all your might! It may still be night
> But already the morning is coming in might!
> Soon the Lord Jesus will come to you, too.

A VOICE FROM THE REAR: There's still work to be had at Mauler's!

Exeunt workers, all but a few women.

JOAN, *gloomily*: Pack up the instruments. Did you see how they hurried away as soon as the soup was gone?
> This thing gets no higher up
> Than the rim of a dish. It believes
> In nothing that it does not
> Hold in its hand – if it believes in hands.
> Living from minute to minute, uncertainly
> They can no longer raise themselves
> From the lowest ground. Only hunger
> Is a match for them. They are touched
> By no song, no word
> Penetrates their depths.

12

To the bystanders.

We Black Straw Hats feel as though we were expected to
satisfy a hungry continent with our spoons.

The workers return. Shouting in the distance.

THE WORKERS, *in front*: What's that yelling? A huge stream of
people from the packing houses!

A VOICE, *at the back*:

Mauler and Cridle are shutting down too!
The Mauler works are locking us out!

THE RETURNING WORKERS:

Running for jobs, we met halfway
A stream of desperate men
Who had lost their jobs and
Asked us for jobs.

THE WORKERS, *in front*:

Alas! From over there, too, a troop of men!
You can't see the end of it! Mauler
Has shut down too! What's to become of us?

THE BLACK STRAW HATS, *to Joan*: Come along with us now.
We're freezing and wet and we have to eat.

JOAN: But now I want to know who's to blame for all this.

THE BLACK STRAW HATS:

Stop! Don't get mixed up in that! They're sure
To give you an earful. Their minds are stuffed
With low ideas! They're lazybones!
Gluttonous, shirkers, from birth onward
Void of all higher impulse!

JOAN: No, I want to know. *To the workers*: Tell me now: why
are you running around here without any work?

THE WORKERS:

Bloody Mauler's locked in battle
With stingy Lennox; so we go hungry.

JOAN: Where does Mauler live?

THE WORKERS:

Over there where livestock is bought and sold
In a big building, the livestock market.

JOAN:

> There I will go, for
> I have to know this.

MARTHA, *one of the Black Straw Hats*:

> Don't get mixed up in that! Ask many questions
> And you'll get lots of answers.

JOAN: No, I want to see this Mauler, who causes such misery.

THE BLACK STRAW HATS:

> Then, Joan, we take a dark view of your further fate.
> Do not mingle in the quarrels of this world!
> He who meddles in a quarrel becomes its victim!
> His purity swiftly perishes. Soon
> His small warmth perishes in the cold
> That reigns over everything. Goodness abandons him
> Who flees the protective hearth.
> Striving downward
> From level to level towards the answer you will never get
> You will disappear in dirt!
> For only dirt is stuffed into the mouths
> Of those who ask without caution.

JOAN: I want to know.

Exeunt Black Straw Hats.

3

PIERPONT MAULER FEELS A BREATH FROM ANOTHER WORLD

In front of the Livestock Market

*Lower level, Joan and Martha waiting; upper level, the meat pack
ers Lennox and Graham, conversing. Lennox is white as chalk.
Noise from the exchange at the rear.*

GRAHAM:
    How you have felt the blows of brutal Mauler
    My good friend Lennox! There's no hindering
    The rise of this monstrosity: to him
    Nature is goods, even the air's for sale.
    What we have inside our stomachs he resells to us.
    He can squeeze rent from ruined houses, money
    From rotten meat; throw stones at him
    He's sure to turn the stones to money; so
    Unruly is his money-lust, so natural
    To him this lack of nature that he himself
    Cannot deny its driving force within him
    For I can tell you: himself, he's soft, does not love money
    Cannot bear squalor, cannot sleep at night.
    Therefore you must approach him as though you could hardly
        speak
    And say: 'Oh, Mauler, look at me and take
    Your hand off my throat – think of your old age – '
    That will frighten him, for sure. Maybe he'll cry . . .
JOAN, *to Martha*:
    Only you, Martha, have followed me this far.
    All the others left me with warnings
    As if I were bound for the end of the world.
    Strange warning from their lips.
    I thank you, Martha.
MARTHA: I warned you too, Joan.
JOAN: And went with me.

MARTHA: But will you really recognize him, Joan?

JOAN: I shall know him!

CRIDLE, *coming out of the building*:

Well, Lennox, now the underbidding's over.
You're finished now and I'll close up and wait
Until the market recovers. I'll clean my yards
And give the knives a thorough oiling and order some
Of those new packing machines that give a fellow
A chance to save a tidy sum in wages.
There's a new system now – the height of cunning.
On a belt of plaited wire, the hog ascends
To the top floor; that's where the slaughtering starts.
Almost unaided, the hog goes plunging down
From the heights onto the knives. You see? The hog
Slaughters itself. And turns itself to sausage.
For now, falling from floor to floor, deserted
By its skin, which is transformed to leather
Then parting from its bristles, which become
Brushes, at last flinging aside its bones –
Flour comes from them – its own weight forces it
All the way down into the can. You see?

GRAHAM:

I see. But what do we do with the can? Accursed times!
Waste lies the market, flooded out by goods.
Trade, that was once so flourishing, lies fallow.
Scuffling over a market that's long been costive
You wrecked your own prices by underbidding one another:
thus
Do buffaloes, fighting for grass, trample to shreds the grass
they fight for.

*Mauler comes out, with his broker, Slift, among a crowd of packers,
two detectives behind him.*

THE MEAT PACKERS:

Now everything's a matter of holding out!

MAULER:

Lennox is down. *To Lennox*: Admit it, you are out.

And now I ask you, Cridle, to take over
The packing plant as stated in our contract
Presuming Lennox finished.

CRIDLE:

Agreed, Lennox is out. But also finished
Are good times on the market; therefore, Mauler
You must come down from ten million for your stock!

MAULER:

What? The price stands
Here in the contract! Here, Lennox, see if this
Is not a contract, with a price right on it!

CRIDLE:

Yes, but a contract made in better times!
Are bad times also mentioned in the contract?
What can I do alone with a stockyard now
When not a soul will buy a can of meat?
Now I know why you couldn't bear to watch
More oxen dying: it was because their flesh
Cannot be sold!

MAULER:

No, it's my heart
That swells, affected by the creatures' shrieks!

GRAHAM:

Oh, mighty Mauler, now I realize
The greatness of your actions: even your heart
Sees far ahead!

LENNOX:

Mauler, I wanted to talk with you ... again ...

GRAHAM:

Straight to his heart, Lennox! Straight to his heart!
It's a sensitive garbage pit!

He hits Mauler in the pit of the stomach.

MAULER: Ouch!

GRAHAM: You see! He *has* a heart!

MAULER:

Well, Freddy, now I'll make a settlement with Cridle

So he can't buy a single can from you
Because you hit me.

GRAHAM:

You can't do that, Pierpy! That's mixing
Personal matters with business.

CRIDLE: O.K., Pierpy, with pleasure. Just as you please.

GRAHAM: I have two thousand workers, Mauler!

CRIDLE: Send them to the movies! But really, Pierpy, our agreement isn't valid. *Figuring in a notebook.* When we contracted for your withdrawal from the business, the shares – of which you hold one-third, as I do – stood at three-ninety. You gave them to me for three-twenty; that was cheap. It's expensive today; they're at a hundred now, because the market's blocked. If I'm to pay you off I'll have to throw the shares onto the market. If I do that they'll go down to seventy, and what can I use to pay you then? Then I'll be done for.

MAULER:

If that's your situation, Cridle, I must certainly
Get my money out of you right away
Before you're done for.
I tell you, Cridle, I am so afraid
I'm all of a sweat, the most I can let you have
Is six days! What am I saying? Five days
If that's your situation.

LENNOX: Mauler, look at me.

MAULER: Lennox, you tell me if the contract says anything about bad times.

LENNOX: No.

Exit.

MAULER, *watching him go*:

Some worry seems to be oppressing him
And I, on business bent (would I were not!)
Did not perceive it! Oh, repulsive business!
Cridle, it sickens me.

Exit Cridle. Meanwhile Joan has called one of the detectives over to her and said something to him.

THE DETECTIVE: Mr Mauler, there are some persons here who
want to talk to you.

MAULER:

Unmannerly lot, eh? With an envious look, eh?

And violent, no doubt? I

Cannot see anyone.

THE DETECTIVE They're a pair from the Black Straw Hat Organization.

MAULER: What kind of an organization is that?

THE DETECTIVE: They have many branches and are numerous
and respected among the lower classes, where they are called
the Good Lord's Soldiers.

MAULER:

I've heard of them. Curious name:

The Good Lord's Soldiers . . . but

What do they want of me?

THE DETECTIVE: They say they have something to discuss with
you.

*During this the market uproar has resumed: Steers 43, Hogs 55,
Heifers 59, etc.*

MAULER:

All right, tell them I will see them.

But tell them also they may say nothing that I

Do not ask about first. Nor must they break out

Into tears or songs, especially sentimental ones.

And tell them it would be most profitable to them

For me to get the impression

That they are well-meaning people, with nothing to their
discredit

Who want nothing from me that I do not have.

Another thing: do not tell them I am Mauler.

THE DETECTIVE, *going over to Joan*:

He consents to see you, but

You must ask no questions, only answer

When he asks you.

JOAN, *walking up to Mauler*: You are Mauler!

MAULER: No, I'm not. *Points to Slift.* That's him.
JOAN, *pointing to Mauler*: You are Mauler.
MAULER: No, he is.
JOAN: You are.
MAULER: How do you know me?
JOAN: Because you have the bloodiest face.

Slift laughs.

MAULER: You laugh, Slift?

Meanwhile Graham has hurried off.

MAULER, *to Joan*: How much do you earn in a day?
JOAN: Twenty cents, but food and clothing are supplied.
MAULER:
  Thin clothes, Slift, and thin soup too, I guess!
  Yes, those clothes are probably thin and the soup not rich.
JOAN:
  Mauler, why do you lock the workers out?
MAULER, *to Slift*:
  The fact that they work without pay
  Is remarkable, isn't it? I never heard
  Of such a thing before – a person working
  For nothing and none the worse. And in their eyes
  I see no fear
  Of being down and out.
To Joan:
  Extraordinary folk, you Black Straw Hats.
  I shall not ask you what particularly
  You want of me. I know the fool mob calls me
  Mauler the Bloody, saying it was I
  Who ruined Lennox or caused unpleasantness
  For Cridle – who, between ourselves, is one
  Of little merit. I can say to you:
  Those are just business matters, and they won't
  Be interesting to you. But there's something else, on which
  I would like to hear your views. I am thinking of giving up
  This bloodstained business, as soon as possible; once for all.

For recently – this *will* interest you – I saw
A steer die and it upset me so
That I want to get rid of everything, and have even sold
My interest in the plant, worth twelve million dollars. I gave
   it to that man
For ten. Don't you feel
That this is right, and to your liking?

SLIFT:

He saw the steer die and made up his mind
To butcher wealthy Cridle
Instead of the poor steer.
Was that right?

The packers laugh.

MAULER:

Go on, laugh. Your laughter's nothing to me. Some day I'll
   see you weep.

JOAN:

Mr Mauler, why have you shut down the stockyards?
This I must know.

MAULER:

Was it not an extraordinary act to take my hand
Out of a mighty concern, simply because it's bloody?
Say this is right, and to your liking.
All right then, don't say it, I know, I admit, some people
Did poorly out of it, they lost their jobs
I know. Unhappily, that was unavoidable.
A bad lot anyway, a tough mob, better not go near them,
   but tell me:
My act in withdrawing my hand from the business
Surely that is right?

JOAN:

I don't know whether you ask in earnest.

MAULER:

That's because my damned voice is used to faking
And for that reason too I know: you
Do not like me. Say nothing.

21

To the others:

I seem to feel a breath from another world wafted towards me.

He takes everybody's money from them and gives it to Joan.

Out with your money, you cattle butchers, give it here!

He takes it out of their pockets, gives it to Joan.

Take it to give to the poor folk, Joan!
But be assured that I feel no obligation in any way
And sleep extremely well. Why am I helping here? Perhaps
Just because I like your face, because it is so unknowing,
   although
You have lived for twenty years.

MARTHA, *to Joan*:

I don't believe in his sincerity.
Forgive me, Joan, for going away now too:
It seems to me you also
Should really drop all this!

Exit Martha.

JOAN: Mr Mauler, you know this is only a drop in the bucket.
   Can you not give them real help?

MAULER:

Tell the world I warmly commend your activities and
Wish there were more like you. But
You mustn't take this thing about the poor this way.
They are wicked people. Human beings do not affect me:
They are not guiltless, and they're butchers themselves. How-
   ever
Let's drop the matter.

JOAN: Mr Mauler, they are saying in the stockyards that you
   are to blame for their misery.

MAULER:

On oxen I have pity; man is evil.
Mankind's not ripe for what you have in mind:
Before the world can change, humanity

Must change its nature.
Wait just one more moment.

In a low tone, to Slift:

Give her more money away from here, when she's alone.
Say 'for the poor folk', so that she can take it
Without blushing, but then see what she buys for herself.
If that's no help – I'd rather it were not –
Then take her with you
To the stockyards and show her
Those poor of hers, how wicked and gross they are, full of
    treachery and cowardice
And how they themselves are to blame.
Maybe that will help.

To Joan:

Here is Sullivan Slift, my broker; he will show you something.

To Slift:

I tell you, it's almost intolerable in my eyes
That there should be people like this girl, owning nothing
But a black hat and twenty cents a day, and fearless.

Exit Mauler.

SLIFT:
I would not care to know what you want to know;
Still, if you wish to know it, come here tomorrow.

JOAN, *watching Mauler go*:
That's not a wicked man, he is the first
To be scared from the tanglewoods of meanness by our drums
The first to hear the call.

SLIFT, *departing*: I give you fair warning: do not take up with
those people down in the yards, they're a lowdown lot, really
the scum of the earth.

JOAN: I want to see it.

4

THE BROKER SULLIVAN SLIFT SHOWS JOAN DARK THE WICKED-
NESS OF THE POOR: JOAN'S SECOND DESCENT INTO THE DEPTHS

The Stockyards District

SLIFT:

Now, Joan, I will show you
The wickedness of those
For whom you feel pity, and
How out of place the feeling is.

*They are walking alongside a factory wall inscribed 'Mauler and
Cridle, Meat Packing Company'. The name Mauler has been painted
out in crosswise strokes. Two men come through a small gate. Slift
and Joan hear their conversation.*

FOREMAN, *to a young apprentice*: Four days ago a man named
Luckerniddle fell into our boiler, we couldn't stop the mach-
inery in time so he got caught in the bacon-maker, a horrible
thing to happen; this is his coat and this is his cap, take them
and get rid of them, all they do is take up a hook in the cloak-
room and make a bad impression. It's a good plan to burn
them, right away would be best. I entrust the things to you
because I know you're a reliable man. I'd lose my job if the
stuff were found anywhere. Of course as soon as the plant
opens again you can have Luckerniddle's job.

THE APPRENTICE: You can count on me, Mr Smith. *The foreman goes back in through the gate.* Too bad about the fellow
that has to go out into the world as bacon, but I feel bad about
his coat too, it's still in good shape. Old Man Bacon has his
can to wear now and won't need this any more, but I could
use it very well. Shit, I'll take it. *Puts it on and wraps his own
coat and cap in newspaper.*

JOAN: I feel sick.

SLIFT: That's the world as it is. *Stopping the young man*: Where-
ever did you get that coat and cap? Didn't they belong to
Luckerniddle, the man that had the accident?

THE APPRENTICE: Please don't let it get around, sir. I'll take the things off right away. I'm pretty nearly down and out. That extra twenty cents you get in the fertilizer-cellars fooled me into working at the bone-grinding machine last year. There I got it bad in the lungs, and a troublesome eye inflammation too. Since then my working capacity has gone down and since February I've only been employed twice.

SLIFT: Keep the things on. And come to Canteen Seven at noon today. You'll get a free lunch and a dollar there if you tell Luckerniddle's wife where your cap and coat came from.

THE APPRENTICE: But, sir, isn't that sort of raw?

SLIFT: Well, if you don't need the money ... !

THE APPRENTICE: You can rely on me, sir.

Joan and Slift walk on.

MRS LUCKERNIDDLE, *sitting in front of the factory gate, lamenting*:
You in there, what are you doing with my husband?
Four days ago he went to work, he said:
'Warm up some soup for me tonight!' And to this
Day he hasn't got back! What have you done with him
You butchers! Four days I have been standing here
In the cold, nights too, waiting, but nobody tells me
Anything, and my husband doesn't come out! But I tell
You, I'm going to stand right here until I get to see him!
You'll rue the day if you've done him any harm!

SLIFT, *walking up to the woman*: Your husband has left town, Mrs Luckerniddle.

MRS LUCKERNIDDLE: Oh, don't give me that again.

SLIFT: I'll tell you something, Mrs Luckerniddle, he is out of town, and it's very embarrassing to the factory to have you sitting around here talking foolishness. So we'll make you an offer which could not be required of us by law. If you give up your search for your husband, you may eat dinner in our canteen every noon for three weeks, free.

MRS LUCKERNIDDLE: I want to know what's become of my husband.

SLIFT: We're telling you, he's gone to Frisco.

MRS LUCKERNIDDLE: He has not gone to Frisco, he's had some accident because of you, and you're trying to hide it.

SLIFT: If that's what you think, Mrs Luckerniddle, you cannot accept any meals from the factory, but you will have to bring suit against the factory. But think it over thoroughly. I shall be at your disposal in the canteen tomorrow. *Slift goes back to Joan.*

MRS LUCKERNIDDLE: I must have my husband back. I have nobody but him to support me.

JOAN:
She will never come.
Twenty dinners may mean much
To one who is hungry, but
He will get more than that.

Joan and Slift walk on. They stop in front of a factory canteen and see two men looking in through a window.

GLOOMB: There sits the overseer who's to blame for my getting my hand in the tin-cutting machine – stuffing his belly full. We must see to it that this is the last time the swine gorges at our expense. You'd better give me your club, mine will probably splinter right off.

SLIFT: Stay here. I want to talk to him. And if he approaches you, say you're looking for work. Then you'll see what kind of people these are. *Going up to Gloomb.* Before you get carried away into doing something – that's the way it looks to me – I'd like to make you a profitable proposition.

GLOOMB: I have no time right now, sir.

SLIFT: That's too bad, because there would have been something in it for you.

GLOOMB: Make it short. We cannot afford to let that swine go. He's got to get his reward today for that inhuman system he plays overseer to.

SLIFT: I have a suggestion to make for your benefit. I am an inspector in the factory. Much inconvenience has been caused by your place remaining vacant. Most people think it too dangerous, just because you have made all this to-do about your fingers. Now it would be just fine if we had someone to fill that post again. If you, for example, could find somebody for it, we would be ready to take you on again right away – in fact, to give you an easier and better paid job than you've had up to now. Perhaps even a foreman's position. You seem a clever man to me. And the one who has it now happens to have got himself disliked lately. You understand. You would also have to take charge of tempo, of course, and above all, as I say, find somebody for that place at the tin-cutting machine, which, I admit, is not safe at all. Over there, for instance, there's a girl looking for work.

GLOOMB: Can a man rely on what you say?

SLIFT: Yes.

GLOOMB: That one over there? She looks weak. It's no job for anyone who tires easily. *To the others*: I've thought it over, we'll do the job tomorrow night. Night's a better time for that kind of fun. So long. *He goes over to Joan.* Looking for a job?

JOAN: Yes.

GLOOMB: Eyesight good?

JOAN: No. Last year I worked at a bone-grinding machine in the fertilizer cellars. I got it bad in the lungs there and a troublesome eye inflammation too. Since then my work-capacity has gone down badly. I've been out of a job since February. Is this a good place?

GLOOMB: The place is good. It's work that even weaker people, like yourself, can do.

JOAN: Are you sure there's no other place to be had? I've heard that working at that machine is dangerous for people who tire easily. Their hands get unsteady and then they grab at the blades.

GLOOMB: That isn't true at all. You'll be surprised to see how pleasant the work is. You'll fan your brow and ask yourself how people could ever tell such silly stories about that machine.

Slift laughs and draws Joan away.

JOAN: Now I'm almost afraid to go on – what will I see next!

They go into the canteen and see Mrs Luckerniddle, who is talking to the waiter.

MRS LUCKERNIDDLE, *figuring*: Twenty dinners ... then I could ... then I'd go and then I'd have ... *She sits down at a table.*

WAITER: If you're not eating you'll have to leave.

MRS LUCKERNIDDLE: I'm waiting for somebody who was going to come in here today or tomorrow. What's for dinner today?

WAITER: Peas.

JOAN:
There she sits.
I thought she was firmly resolved, and feared
That she still might come tomorrow, and now she has run here faster than we
And is here already, waiting for us.

SLIFT: Go and take her the food yourself – maybe she'll think again.

Joan fetches a plate of food and brings it to Mrs Luckerniddle.

JOAN: Here so soon?

MRS LUCKERNIDDLE: It's because I've had nothing to eat for two days.

JOAN: You didn't know we were coming in today, did you?

MRS LUCKERNIDDLE: That's right.

JOAN: On the way over here I heard someone say that something happened to your husband in the factory and the factory is responsible.

MRS LUCKERNIDDLE: Oh, so you've reconsidered your offer? So I don't get my twenty meals?

JOAN: But you got along with your husband very well, didn't you? People told me you have nobody except him.

MRS LUCKERNIDDLE: Well, I've had nothing to eat for two days.

JOAN: Won't you wait till tomorrow? If you give up your husband now, no one will ask after him any more.

Mrs. Luckerniddle is silent.

Don't take it.

Mrs Luckerniddle snatches the food from her hand and begins to eat greedily.

MRS LUCKERNIDDLE: He's gone to Frisco.
JOAN:

And basements and storerooms are full of meat
That cannot be sold and is going rotten
Because no one will take it away.

The worker with the cap and the coat enters, rear.

THE WORKER: Good morning, is this where I eat?
SLIFT: Just take a seat beside that woman over there.

The man sits down.

That's a good-looking cap you have there.

The worker hides it.

Where did you get it?
THE WORKER: Bought it.
SLIFT: Well, where did you buy it?
THE WORKER: Not in any store.
SLIFT: Then where did you get it?
THE WORKER: I got it off a man that fell into a boiling vat.

Mrs Luckerniddle feels sick. She gets up and goes out. On the way she says to the waiter:

MRS LUCKERNIDDLE: Leave the plate where it is. I'm coming back. I'm coming here for dinner every day. Just ask that gentleman.

Exit.

SLIFT: For three whole weeks she will come and feed, without looking up, like an animal. Have you seen, Joan, that their wickedness is beyond measure?
JOAN:

But what mastery you have
Over their wickedness! How you thrive on it!
Do you not see that it rains on their wickedness?

29

Certainly she would have liked
To be true to her husband, as others are
And to ask after the man who supported her
For some time longer, as is proper.
But the price was too high: it amounted to twenty meals.
And would that young man on whom
Any scoundrel can rely
Have shown the coat to the dead man's wife
If things had gone as he would like?
But the price appeared too high to him.
And why would the man with only one arm
Have failed to warn me? If the price
Of so small a scruple were not so high for him?
Why, instead, did he sell his wrath, which is righteous, but
    too dear?
If their wickedness is beyond measure, then
So is their poverty. Not the wickedness of the poor
Have you shown me, but
The poverty of the poor.
You've shown the evil of the poor to me:
Now see the woes of evil poverty.
O thoughtless rumour, that the poor are base:
You shall be silenced by their stricken face!

JOAN INTRODUCES THE POOR TO THE LIVESTOCK EXCHANGE

The Livestock Exchange

THE PACKERS:

We have canned meat for sale!
Wholesalers, buy canned meat!
Fresh, juicy canned meat!
Mauler and Cridle's bacon!
Graham's sirloins, soft as butter!
Wilde's Kentucky lard, a bargain!

THE WHOLESALERS:

And silence fell upon the waters and
Bankruptcy among the wholesalers!

THE PACKERS:

Due to tremendous technical advances
Engineers' hard work and entrepreneurs' farsightedness
We have now succeeded
In lowering prices for
Mauler and Cridle's bacon
Graham's sirloins, soft as butter
Wilde's Kentucky lard, a bargain
BY ONE-THIRD!
Wholesalers, buy canned meat!
Seize your opportunity!

THE WHOLESALERS:

And silence fell upon the mountaintops
And hotel kitchens covered their heads
And stores looked away in horror
And middlemen turned pale!
We wholesalers vomit if we so much as
See a can of meat. This country's stomach
Has eaten too much meat from cans
And is fighting back.

SLIFT:

What news from your friends in New York?

MAULER:

Theories. If they had their way
The meat ring would be lying in the gutter
And stay there for weeks till there wasn't a peep left in it
And I'd have all that meat around my neck!
Madness!

SLIFT:

I'd have to laugh if those men in New York really had
Tariffs lowered now, opened up the South
And started a bull market – just supposing! – and we
Were to miss the bus!

MAULER:

What if they did? Would you be harsh enough
To hack your pound of flesh from misery
Like this? Look at them, watching for a move
As lynxes do! I couldn't be so harsh.

THE WHOLESALERS:

Here we stand, wholesalers with mountains of cans
And cellars full of frozen steers
Wanting to sell the steers in cans
And no one will buy them!
And our customers, the kitchens and stores
Are stuffed to the ceiling with frozen meat!
Screaming for buyers and eaters!
No more buying for us!

THE PACKERS:

Here we stand, packers with slaughter-houses and packing
    space
And stables full of steers; day and night the machines
Run on under steam; brine, tubs and boiling vats
Wanting to turn the lowing ravenous herds
Into canned meat and nobody wants canned meat.
We're ruined.

THE STOCKBREEDERS:

And what about us, the stockbreeders?
Who'll buy livestock now? In our stables stand
Steers and hogs eating expensive corn

And they ride to town in trains and while they ride
They eat and eat and at stations
They wait in rent-devouring boxcars, forever eating.

MAULER:

And now the knives motion them back
Death, giving livestock the cold shoulder
Closes his shop.

THE PACKERS, *shouting at Mauler, who is reading a newspaper*:

Traitorous Mauler, nest-befouler!
Do you think we don't know who's selling livestock here –
Oh so secretly – and knocking the bottom out of prices?
You've been offering meat for days and days!

MAULER:

Insolent butchers, cry in your mothers' laps
Because the hunted creature's outcry ceases!
Go home and say that one of all your number
Could not hear oxen bellow any longer
And would rather hear your bellow than their bellow!
I want my cash and quiet for my conscience!

A BROKER, *bellowing from the Exchange entrance, at the rear*:

Terrific drop in stock exchange quotations!
Colossal sales of stocks. Cridle, formerly Mauler
Whirl the whole meat-ring's rates down with them
Into the abyss.

Uproar arises among the meat packers. They rush at Cridle, who is white as chalk.

THE PACKERS:

What's the meaning of this, Cridle? Look us in the eye!
Dumping stocks, with the market the way it is?

THE BROKERS:

At a hundred and fifteen!

THE PACKERS:

Are your brains made of dung?
It's not yourself alone you're ruining!
You big shit! You criminal!

CRIDLE, *pointing to Mauler*:

There's your man!

GRAHAM, *standing in front of Cridle*:

This isn't Cridle's doing, someone else
Is fishing these waters and we're supposed to be the fish!
There are people who want to take care of the meat-ring, now
And do a final job! Defend yourself, Mauler!

THE PACKERS, *to Mauler*:

The story is, Mauler, that you're squeezing your money
Out of Cridle, who, we hear, is groggy already, and Cridle
Himself says nothing and points to you.

MAULER: If I leave my money in this Cridle's hands an hour longer – a man who's confessed to me personally that he's lazy – who among you would still take me seriously as a businessman? And I want nothing so much as for *you* to take me seriously.

CRIDLE, *to the bystanders*: Just four weeks ago I made a contract with Mauler. He wanted to sell me his shares – one-third of the total – for ten million dollars. From that time on, as I've just found out, he has been secretly selling quantities of livestock, cheap, to make a still worse mess of prices that are sagging already. He could ask for his money whenever he wanted to. I intended to pay him by disposing of part of his shares on the market – they were high then – and reinvesting part. Then the drop came. Today Mauler's shares are worth not ten but three million. The whole plant is worth ten million instead of thirty. That's exactly the ten million I owe Mauler, and that's what he wants overnight.

THE PACKERS:

If you're doing this, making things hard for Cridle
Whose in-laws we are not, then you're well aware
That this concerns us too. You're stripping
All business bare: the fault is yours
If our cans of meat are as cheap as sand
Because you ruined Lennox with cheap cans!

MAULER:

You shouldn't have gone and slaughtered so many cattle

You raving butchers! Now I want my money;
Though you should all go begging, I must have
My money! I have other plans.

THE STOCKBREEDERS: Lennox smashed! And Cridle groggy!
And Mauler pulls all his money out!

THE SMALL SPECULATORS:
Oh, as for us, the little speculators
Nobody cares. They scream when they see
The colossus topple, but don't see where it falls
Whom it strikes down. Mauler! Our money!

THE PACKERS: Eighty thousand cans at fifty, but fast!

THE WHOLESALERS: Not a single one!

Silence.

The drumming of the Black Straw Hats and Joan's voice are heard.

JOAN: Pierpont Mauler! Where is Mauler?

MAULER:
What's that drumming? Who
Is calling my name?
Here, where every man
Shows his bare chops all smeared with blood!

The Black Straw Hats march in. They sing their war-chant.

THE BLACK STRAW HATS, *singing*:
Attention, pay attention!
There is a man who's falling!
There is a cry for help!
There is a woman calling!
Halt the autos, stop all traffic!
Men falling all around us and no one looks their way!
Is there no sight in your eye?
Say hello to your brother, not just any guy!
Get up from where you've dined –
Is there no thought in your mind
For the starving folk nearby?
I hear you say: it will always be the same
The injustice of the world will still remain.

But we say this to you: You've got to march
And leave your cares and help with might and main
And bring up tanks and cannon too
And airplanes there shall be
And battleships over the sea
To conquer a plate of soup, poor brother, just for you.
You've all got to lend a hand
And it must be today
For the army of the good
Is not a vast array.
Forward march! Eyes right! Rifles ready to fire!
Men falling all around us and no one looks their way!

Meanwhile the Exchange battle has continued. But laughter, prompted by exclamations, is spreading towards the front of the scene.

THE PACKERS: Eighty thousand cans at half price, but fast!
THE WHOLESALERS: Not a single one!
THE PACKERS: Then we're finished, Mauler!
JOAN: Where is Mauler?
MAULER:

Don't go, Slift! Graham, Meyers
Stay there in front of me.
I don't want to be seen here.

THE STOCKBREEDERS:

Not a steer to be sold in Chicago any more.
This day spells ruin for all of Illinois
With mounting prices you prodded us on into raising steers
And here we stand with steers
And no one will buy them.
Mauler, you hound, you are to blame for this disaster.

MAULER:

Enough of business. Graham! My hat. I've got to go.
A hundred dollars for my hat.

CRIDLE: Oh, damn you to hell.

Exit Cridle.

JOAN: Now, you stay here, Mr Mauler, and listen to what I have to say to you. It is something you all may hear. Quiet! Yes, indeed, you hardly think it right for us Black Straw Hats to turn up like this in the dark hidden places where you do your business! I've been told about the kind of things you do here, how you make meat more and more expensive by your carryings-on and subtle trickery. But if you ever supposed you could keep it all concealed, then you're on the wrong track, now and on the Day of Judgment, for then it will be revealed, and how will you look then, when our Lord and Saviour has you walk up in a row and asks with His big eyes, 'Well, where are my steers? What have you done with them? Did you make them available to the people at prices within their reach? What has become of them, then?' And when you stand there embarrassed, groping for excuses, the way you do in your newspapers, which don't always stick to the truth, then the steers will bellow at your backs in all the barns where you keep them tucked away to make prices go sky-high, and by their bellowing they will bear witness against you before Almighty God!

Laughter.

THE STOCKBREEDERS:
We stockbreeders see nothing funny in that!
Dependent on weather, summer and winter, we stand
Considerably nearer the Lord of old.

JOAN: And now an example. If a man builds a dam against the unreasonable water, and a thousand people help him with the labour of their hands, and he gets a million for it, but the dam breaks as soon as the water rises and everybody working on it and many more are drowned – what kind of man is he who builds a dam like that? You may call him a businessman or a rascal, depending on your views, but we tell you he's a numskull. And all you men who make bread dear and life a hell for human beings, so that they all become devils, you are numskulls, wretched, stingy numskulls and nothing else!

THE WHOLESALERS, *shouting*:
Because of your irresponsible

Juggling with prices and filthy lust for profit
You're bringing on your own ruin!
Numskulls!

THE PACKERS, *shouting back*:

Numskulls yourselves!
Nothing can be done about crises!
Unshakable above our heads
Stands economic law, the not-to-be-known.
Terrible is the cyclic recurrence
Of natural catastrophes!

THE STOCKBREEDERS:

Nothing to be done about our hold on your throats?
That's wickedness, barefaced lying wickedness!

JOAN: And why does this wickedness exist in the world? Well,
how could it be otherwise? Naturally, if a man has to smash
his neighbour's head for a ham sandwich so that he can
satisfy his elementary needs, brother striving with brother
for the bare necessities of life, how can the sense of higher
things help being stifled in the human heart? Why not think
of helping your neighbour simply as serving a customer?
Then you'll understand the New Testament in a flash, and
see how fundamentally modern it is, even today. Service!
Why, what does service mean if not charity – in the true
meaning of the word, that is! Gentlemen, I keep hearing that
the poor haven't enough morals, and it's true, too. Immorality
makes its nest down there in the slums, with revolution itself
for company. I simply ask you: Where are they to get morals
from, if they have nothing else? Where can they get anything
without stealing it? Gentlemen, there is such a thing as moral
purchasing-power.Raise moral purchasing-power, and there's
your morality. And I mean by purchasing-power a very simple and natural thing – that is, money, wages. And this
brings me back to the practical point: if you go on like this
you'll end by eating your own meat, because the people outside haven't got any purchasing power.

THE STOCKBREEDERS, *reproachfully*:

Here we stand with steers

And nobody can afford them.

JOAN: But you sit here, you great and mighty men, thinking that
no one will ever catch on to your tricks, and refusing to know
anything about the misery in the world outside. Well then,
just take a look at them, the people whom your treatment has
brought to this condition, the people you will not admit to be
your brothers! Come out now, you weary and heavy-laden,
into the light of day. Don't be ashamed! *Joan shows to the
Exchange crowd the poor people she has brought along with her.*

MAULER, *shouting*: Take them away! *He faints.*

A VOICE, *rear*: Pierpont Mauler has fainted!

THE POOR PEOPLE: He's the one to blame for everything!

The packers attend to Mauler.

THE PACKERS: Water for Pierpont Mauler!

A doctor for Mauler!

JOAN:

If you, Mauler, showed me the wickedness

Of the poor, now I show you

The poverty of the poor, for they live far away from you

And that puts beyond their reach goods they cannot do without –

The people out of sight, whom you

Hold down in poverty like this, so weakened and so urgently

In need of unobtainable food and warmth that they

Can be just as far away from any claim

To higher things than the lowest gluttony, the beastliest
habits.

Mauler comes to.

MAULER: Are they still here? I implore you, send them away.

THE PACKERS: The Black Straw Hats? You want them sent
away?

MAULER: No, those others, behind them.

SLIFT: He won't open his eyes before they get out.

GRAHAM:

Can't bring yourself to look at them, eh? But it was you

Who brought them to this state.

Shutting your eyes won't rid you of them
Far from it.

MAULER:

I beseech you, send them away! I'll buy!
Listen, all of you: Pierpont Mauler's buying!
So that these people may get work and go.
Eight weeks' production in cans of meat –
I'll buy it!

THE PACKERS: He's bought! Mauler has bought!

MAULER: At today's prices!

GRAHAM, *holding him up*: And what about back stocks?

MAULER, *lying on the floor*: I'll buy 'em.

GRAHAM: At fifty?

MAULER: At fifty.

GRAHAM: He's bought! You heard it, he has bought!

THE BROKERS, *shouting through megaphones, at the rear*: Pierpont
Mauler keeps the meat market going. According to contract,
he's taking over the meat-ring's entire stock, at fifty, as of
today, besides two months' production, starting today, also
at fifty. The meat-ring will deliver at least four hundred tons
of canned meat to Pierpont Mauler on November fifteenth.

MAULER: But now, my friends, I beg you, take me away.

Mauler is carried out.

JOAN:

That's fine, now have yourself carried out!
We work at our mission jobs like plough-horses
And this is the kind of thing you do up here!
You had your man tell me I shouldn't say a thing.
Who are you, I'd like to know
To try to muzzle the Lord in His goodness? You shouldn't
even
Muzzle the ox that's yoked to the thresher!
And speak I will.

To the poor people:

You'll have work again on Monday.

THE POOR PEOPLE: We've never seen such people anywhere. But we'd prefer them to the two that were standing beside him. They have a far worse look than he does.

JOAN: Now sing, as a farewell song, *Who Ever feels the Lack of Bread*.

THE BLACK STRAW HATS, *singing*:

Who ever feels the lack of bread
Once he's given the Lord his bond?
A man will never be in need
If he stays within God's grace.
For how shall snow fall on him there?
And how shall hunger find that place?

THE WHOLESALERS:

The fellow's sick in his head. This country's stomach
Has eaten too much meat from cans and it's fighting back.
And he has meat put into cans
That no one will buy. Cross out his name!

THE STOCKBREEDERS:

Come on, up with those prices, you lousy butchers!
Until you double livestock prices
Not an ounce will be delivered, for you need it.

THE PACKERS:

Keep your filth to yourselves! We will not buy.
For the contract which you saw agreed on here
Is a mere scrap of paper. The man who made it
Was not in his right mind. He couldn't raise
A cent from Frisco to New York
For that kind of business.

Exeunt packers.

JOAN: Well, anyone who is really interested in God's word and what He says and not just in what the ticker tape says, and there must be some people here that are respectable and conduct their business in a God-fearing way, we have nothing against that – well, he's welcome to visit our Divine Service Sunday afternoon in Lincoln Street at two o'clock. Music from three o'clock, no entrance charge.

SLIFT, *to the stockbreeders*:

What Pierpont Mauler promises he fulfils.
Breathe freely now! The market's getting well!
You who give bread and you to whom it's given
At last the doldrums have been overcome!
They menaced confidence, and even concord.
You who give work, and you to whom it's given
You're moving in and opening wide the gates!
Sensible counsel, sensibly adopted
Has got the upper hand of foolishness.
The gates are opening! The chimney's smoking!
It's work you've both been needing all the time.

THE STOCKBREEDERS, *placing Joan up on the steps*:

Your speech and presence made a great impression
On us stockbreeders and many a man
Was deeply moved, for we
Have terrible sufferings too.

JOAN:

You know, I have my eye
On Mauler, he has woken you up, and you
If there's something you need to help you out
Then come with me, that he may aid you also
For from now on he shall not rest
Till everyone is helped.
For he's in a position to help: so
Let's go after him.

Exeunt Joan and Black Straw Hats, followed by the stockbreeders.

THE CRICKET CAUGHT

The City. The broker Sullivan Slift's house,
a small one with two entrances

MAULER, *inside the house, talking to Slift*: Lock the door, turn on
  all the lights there are – then take a good look at my face,
  Slift, and see if it's true that anybody could tell by it.

SLIFT: Tell what by it?

MAULER: My business!

SLIFT: A butcher's? Mauler, why did you fall down when she
  talked?

MAULER:

  What did she say? I did not hear it

  For behind her there stood such people with such ghastly
      faces

  Of misery – misery that comes

  Before a wrath that will sweep us all away –

  That I saw nothing more. Slift

  I will tell you what I really think

  About this business of ours.

  It can't go on this way, nothing but buying and selling

  And one man coldly stripping off another's skin:

  There are too many people howling with pain

  And they are on the increase.

  That which falls into our bloody cellars

  Is past all consolation:

  When they get hold of us they'll slap us against the pavement

  Like rotten fish. All of us here

  We're not going to die in our beds. Before

  We get that far they will stand us up against walls

  In throngs and cleanse the world of us and

  Our hangers-on.

SLIFT: They have upset you! *Aside*: I'll make him eat a rare
  steak. His old weakness has come over him again. Maybe he'll

come to his senses after enjoying some raw meat. *He goes and broils Mauler a steak on a gas stove.*

MAULER:

I often ask myself why
I'm moved by that fool talk, worlds away
The cheap, flat chitter-chatter they study up ...
Of course, it's because they do it for nothing, eighteen hours
    a day and
In rain and hunger.

SLIFT:

In cities which are burning down below
And freezing up on top, there are always people
Who'll talk of this and that – details that aren't
In perfect order.

MAULER:

But what is it they're saying? In these cities, incessantly
On fire, in the downward rush
Of howling humanity,
Surging towards hell without respite
For years on end, if I hear a voice like that –
Foolish, of course, but quite unlike a beast's –
I feel as if I'd been cracked on the backbone with a stick
Like a leaping fish.
But even this has only been evasion until now, Slift
For what I fear is something other than God.

SLIFT: What is it?

MAULER:

Not what is above me
But what is below me! What stands in the stockyards and
cannot last through the night and will still – I know – rise up
in the morning.

SLIFT: Won't you eat a little meat, my dear Pierpont? Think,
now you can do it with a clear conscience again, for from this
day onward you won't have anything to do with cattle-
slaughtering.

MAULER:

Do you think I should? Perhaps I could.

I ought to be able to eat now, oughtn't I?

SLIFT: Have a bite to eat and think over your situation. It's not very satisfactory. Do you realize that today you bought up everything there is in cans?

Mauler, I see you engrossed in the contemplation of your noble nature, allow me to give you a concise account of your situation, the external, the unimportant one.

The main point is that you've taken one hundred and fifty tons of stocks away from the meat-ring. You'll have to get rid of these in the next few weeks on a market that can't swallow one more can even today. You've paid fifty for them, but the price will go down at least to thirty. On November fifteenth, when the price is thirty or twenty-five, the meat-ring will deliver four hundred tons to you at fifty.

MAULER:

Slift! I'm done for!

I'm finished. I've gone and bought up meat.

Oh, Slift, what have I done!

Slift, I've loaded myself with all the meat in the world.

Like Atlas I stumble, cans by the ton on my shoulders

All the way down to join the people who sleep

Under bridges. Only this morning

Many men were about to fall, and I

Went to see them fall and laugh at them

And tell them not a soul

Would be fool enough to buy meat in cans now

And while I stand there I hear my own voice saying:

I'll buy it all.

Slift, I've gone and bought meat, I'm done for.

SLIFT: Well, what do you hear from your friends in New York?

MAULER: That I ought to buy meat.

SLIFT: You ought to do what?

MAULER: Buy meat.

SLIFT Then why are you yammering because you have bought it?

MAULER: Yes, they told me I ought to buy meat.

SLIFT: But you have bought meat!

MAULER:

> Yes, that is so, I did buy meat, but I bought it
> Not because of the letter that said I should
> (That's all wrong anyhow, just armchair theory)
> Not from any low motives, but because
> That person gave me such a shock, I swear
> I barely riffled through the letter, it only came this morning.
> Here it is. 'Dear Pierpont —

SLIFT *reads on*: – today we are able to inform you that our money
is beginning to bear fruit. Many congressmen are going to
vote against tariffs, so it seems advisable to buy meat, dear
Pierpont. We shall write you again tomorrow.'

MAULER:

> This bribery, too, is something
> That shouldn't happen. How easily a war
> Might start from a thing like that, and thousands bleed
> For filthy lucre. Oh, my dear Slift, I feel
> That nothing good can come of news like this.

SLIFT:

> That would depend on who had written the letters.
> Bribing, abolishing tariffs, making wars –
> Not everybody can do that. Are these people all right?

MAULER: They're solvent.

SLIFT: But who are they?

Mauler smiles.

> Then prices might go even higher still?
> Then we'd be sitting pretty after all.
> That might be a prospect if it wasn't for the farmers –
> By offering all their meat, only too eagerly
> They'd bring prices crashing down again. No, Mauler
> I don't understand that letter.

MAULER:

> Think of it this way: a man has committed theft
> And is caught by a man.
> Now if he doesn't knock the other man down
> He's done for; if he does, he's out of the woods.

The letter (which is wrong) demands (so as to be right)
A misdeed like that.

SLIFT: What misdeed?

MAULER:

The kind I could never commit. For from now on
I wish to live in peace. If they want to profit
By their misdeeds – and they will profit –
They need only buy up meat wherever they see it
Beat into the stockbreeders' heads the fact
That there's too much meat around and mention
The flattening of Lennox and take
Their meat away from them. This above all:
Take the stockbreeders' meat from them . . . but then
They'll be duped all over again . . . no, I'll have nothing
To do with that.

SLIFT:

You shouldn't have bought meat, Pierpont.

MAULER:

Yes, it's a bad business, Slift.
I'm not going to buy so much as a hat or a shoe
Until I get out of this mess, and I'll be happy
If I have a hundred dollars when I do.

Sound of drums. Joan approaches, with the stockbreeders.

JOAN: We'll lure him out of his building the way you catch a
cricket. You stand over there, because if he hears us singing
he'll try to get out the other way, to avoid meeting me again:
I'm a person he doesn't care to see. *She laughs.* And so are
the people who are with me.

The stockbreeders take up a position in front of the door, right.

JOAN, *in front of the door, left*: Please come out, Mr Mauler, I
must talk to you about the terrible condition of the stockbreeders of Illinois. I also have several workers with me – they
want to ask you when you're going to reopen your factory.

MAULER: Slift, where's the other exit? I don't want to run into
her again, still less the people she has with her. I'm not opening any factories now, either.

47

SLIFT: Come out this way.

They go through the interior to door, right.

THE STOCKBREEDERS, *in front of door, left*: Come on out, Mauler, our troubles are all your fault, and we are more than ten thousand Illinois stockbreeders who don't know whether we're coming or going. So buy our livestock from us!

MAULER:

Shut the door, Slift! I'm not buying.

With the whole world's canned meat around my neck

Now should I buy the cattle on the dog-star?

It's as if a man should go to Atlas when

He can barely drag the world along, and say:

'They need another carrier on Saturn.'

Who's going to buy the livestock back from me?

SLIFT: The Grahams, most likely – they need it!

JOAN, *in front of the door, left*: We're not leaving this place until the stockbreeders get some help.

MAULER: Most likely the Grahams, yes, they need livestock. Slift, go out and tell them to let me have two minutes to think things over.

Slift goes.

SLIFT, *to the stockbreeders*: Pierpont Mauler wishes to give careful consideration to your request. He asks for two minutes' thinking time.

Slift re-enters the house.

MAULER: I'm not buying. *He starts figuring.* Slift, I'm buying. Slift, bring me anything that looks like a hog or a steer, I'll buy it, whatever smells of lard, I'll buy it, bring every speck of fat, I'm the buyer for it, and at today's price too, at fifty.

SLIFT:

Not a hat will you buy, Mauler, but

All the cattle in Illinois.

MAULER:

Yes, I'll still buy that. Now it's decided, Slift.

Take A.

He draws an A on a closet door.

> A man does something wrong, let that be A
> He did it because his feelings overcame him
> And now he goes on to do B, and B's wrong too
> And now the sum of A and B is right.
> Ask the stockbreeders in, they're very nice people
> Badly in need and decently clothed and not
> The sort of folk that scare you when you see them.

SLIFT, *stepping out in front of the house, to the stockbreeders*: To save Illinois and avert ruin from its farmers and stockbreeders, Pierpont Mauler has decided to buy up all the livestock on the market. But the contracts are not to run in his name, because his name may not be mentioned.

THE STOCKBREEDERS: Long live Pierpont Mauler! He's saved the livestock trade!

They enter the house.

JOAN, *calling after them*: Tell Mr Mauler that we, the Black Straw Hats, thank him for this in the name of the Lord. *To the workers*: If the people who buy cattle and the people who sell cattle are satisfied, then there'll be bread once more for you too.

THE EXPULSION OF THE MONEY-CHANGERS
FROM THE TEMPLE

The Black Straw Hats' Mission

The Black Straw Hats, sitting at a long table, are counting out from their tin boxes the widows' and orphans' mites they have collected.

THE BLACK STRAW HATS, *singing*:
> Gather the pennies of widows and orphans with song!
> Great is the need
> They have no roof or bread
> But Almighty God
> Won't let them go hungry long.

PAULUS SNYDER, *Major of the Black Straw Hats, getting up*: Very little, very little. *To some poor folk in the background, among them Mrs Luckerniddle and Gloomb*: You here again? Don't you ever leave this place? There's work at the stockyards again, you know!

MRS LUCKERNIDDLE: Where? The yards are shut down.

GLOOMB: We were told they would open up again, but they haven't.

SNYDER: Well, don't go too near the cash-box. *He motions them still further back.*

Mulberry, the landlord, enters.

MULBERRY: Say, what about my rent?

SNYDER: My dear Black Straw Hats, my dear Mulberry, my honoured listeners! As to this troublesome problem of financing our operations – anything that's good speaks for itself, and needs propaganda more than anything – hitherto we have aimed our appeals at the poor, indeed the poorest, on the assumption that they, being most in need of God's help, were the people most likely to have a bit left over for Him, and that their sheer numbers would produce the desired effect. To our regret, it has been borne in upon us that these very classes

manifest an attitude of reserve towards God that is quite beyond explanation. Of course, this may be due to the fact that
they have nothing. Therefore, I, Paulus Snyder, have issued
an invitation in your name to Chicago's wealthy and pros-
perous citizens, to help us launch a major offensive next
Sunday against the unbelief and materialism of the city of
Chicago, primarily among the lower orders. Out of the pro-
ceeds we shall also pay our dear landlord, Mr Mulberry, the
rent he is so kindly deferring for us.

MULBERRY: It would certainly be very welcome, but please don't
worry about it.

Exit.

SNYDER: Well, now go happily about your work and be sure to
clean the front steps.

Exeunt Black Straw Hats.

SNYDER: Tell me, are the locked-out workers in the stockyards
still standing there patiently, or have they begun to talk like
rebels?

MRS LUCKERNIDDLE: They've been squawking pretty loud since
yesterday, because they know the factories are getting orders.

GLOOMB: Many are saying already that they won't get any more
work at all if they don't use force.

SNYDER, *to himself*: A good sign. The meat kings will be more
likely to come and listen to our appeal if they're driven in by
stones. *To the poor people*: Couldn't you split our wood, at
least?

THE POOR PEOPLE: There isn't any more, Major.

Enter the packers Cridle, Graham, Meyers, and the broker Slift.

MEYERS: You know, Graham, I keep asking myself where that
livestock can be hiding out.

GRAHAM: That's what I'm asking too, where can that livestock
be hiding out?

SLIFT: So am I.

GRAHAM: Oh, you too? And I guess Mauler is too, eh?

SLIFT: I guess he is.

MEYERS:

> Somewhere some swine is buying everything up.
> Someone who knows quite well that we're committed
> By contract to deliver meat in cans
> And so need livestock.

SLIFT: Who can it be?

GRAHAM, *hitting him in the stomach*:

> You cur, you!
> Don't play any tricks on us there, and tell Pierpy not to either!
> That's a vital spot!

SLIFT, *to Snyder*: What do you want of us?

GRAHAM, *hitting him again*: What do you think they want, Slift?

Slift, with exaggerated mockery, makes the gesture of handing out money.

> You said it, Slift!

MEYERS, *to Snyder*: Fire away.

They sit down on the prayer benches.

SNYDER, *in the pulpit*: We Black Straw Hats have heard that fifty thousand men are standing around in the stockyards without work. And that some are beginning to grumble and say: 'We'll have to help ourselves.' Aren't your names beginning to be called as the ones to blame for fifty thousand men being out of work and standing idly in front of the factories? They'll end by taking the factories away from you and saying: 'We'll act the way the Bolsheviks did and take the factories into our own hands so that everybody can work and eat.' For the story is getting around that unhappiness doesn't just come like the rain but is made by certain persons who get profit out of it. But we Black Straw Hats try to tell them that unhappiness does come down like the rain, and no one knows where from, and that they are destined to suffering and there's a reward for it shining at the end of the road.

THE PACKERS: Why mention rewards?

SNYDER: The reward we speak of is paid out after death.

THE PACKERS: How much will it cost?

SNYDER: Eight hundred dollars a month, because we need hot soup and loud music. We also want to promise them that the rich will be punished – when they're dead, of course. *The packers laugh noisily.* All that for a mere eight hundred a month!

GRAHAM: You don't need that much, man. Five hundred.

SNYDER: Well, we could get along with seven hundred and fifty, but then –

MEYERS: Seven hundred and fifty. That's better. Let's make it five hundred.

GRAHAM: You do need five hundred, certainly. *To the others*: They've got to get that.

MEYERS: Out with it, Slift, you fellows have that livestock.

SLIFT: Mauler and I have not bought one cent's worth of livestock, as true as I'm sitting here. The Lord's my witness.

MEYERS, *to Snyder*: Five hundred dollars, eh? That's a lot of money. Who's going to pay it?

SLIFT: Yes, you'll have to find someone who will give it to you.

SNYDER: Yes, yes.

MEYERS: That won't be easy.

GRAHAM: Come on, Slift, cough it up, Pierpy has the livestock.

SLIFT, *laughing*: A bunch of crooks, Mr Snyder.

All laugh except Snyder.

GRAHAM, *to Meyers*: The man has no sense of humour. Don't like him.

SLIFT: The main point is, man, where do you stand? On this side of the barricades, or the other?

SNYDER: The Black Straw Hats stand above the battle, Mr Slift. This side.

Enter Joan.

SLIFT: Why, here's our sainted Joan of the Livestock Exchange!

THE THREE PACKERS, *shouting at Joan*: We're not satisfied with you, can't you tell Mauler something from us? You're supposed to have some influence with him. They say he eats out of your hand. Well, the market is so short of livestock that we have to keep an eye on him. They say you can bring him round to doing whatever you want. Have him get that livestock out. Listen, if you'll do this for us we're willing to pay the Black Straw Hat's rent for the next four years.

Joan has seen the poor people and is shocked.

JOAN: Why, what are you doing here?

MRS LUCKERNIDDLE, *coming forward*:
The twenty dinners are all eaten now.
Please don't get angry because I'm here again.
It's a sight I would be glad enough to spare you.
That's the awful thing about hunger: no sooner
Is it satisfied than back it comes again.

GLOOMB, *coming forward*:
I know you, it was you I tried to talk
Into working on that slicer that tore my arm off.
I could do worse things than that today.

JOAN: Why aren't you working? I did get work for you.

MRS LUCKERNIDDLE: Where? The stockyards are closed.

GLOOMB: We were told they would open up again, but they haven't.

JOAN, *to the packers*:
So they're still waiting, are they?

The packers say nothing.

And I thought they had been provided for!
It's been snowing on them now for seven days
And the very snow that kills them cuts them off
From every human eye. How easily
I forgot what everyone likes to forget for the peace of his mind!
If one man says things are all right again, no one looks into
    them.

To the packers.

But surely Mauler bought meat from you? He did it at my request! And now you still refuse to open up your factories?

CRIDLE, GRAHAM, MEYERS: That's quite right, we wanted to open up.

SLIFT: But first of all you wanted to leap at the farmers' throats!

CRIDLE, GRAHAM, MEYERS: How are we to do any slaughtering when there's no livestock?

SLIFT: When Mauler and I bought meat from you we took it for granted you would start employment going again so that the workers would be able to buy meat. Now who will eat the meat we got from you? For whom did we buy meat if the consumers can't pay for it?

JOAN: Look, if you people have control of all the equipment your employees use in your all-powerful factories and plants, then the least you could do would be to let them in, if they're kept out it's all up with them, because there is a sort of exploitation about the whole thing, and if a poor human creature is tormented till the blood comes, and can think of no way out but to take a club and bash his tormentor's head in, then it scares the daylights out of you, I've noticed that, and then you think religion's fine and it's supposed to pour oil on the troubled waters, but the Lord has His pride too, and He won't pitch in and clean your pigsties for you all over again. And I run around from pillar to post, thinking: 'If I help you people on top, the people under you will also be helped. It's all one in a way, and the same strings pull it,' but I was a prize fool there. If a man wants to help folks that are poor it seems he'd better help them get away from you. Is there no respect left in you for anything that wears a human face? Some day, maybe, you won't rate as human beings either, but as wild animals that will simply have to be slaughtered in the interest of public order and safety! And still you have the confidence to enter the house of God, just because you own that filthy Mammon, everybody knows where you got it and how, it wasn't come by honestly. But this time, by God, you've come to the wrong people, we'll have to drive you out, that's all, yes, drive you out with a stick. Come on, don't stand there looking so stupid, I know human beings shouldn't be treated like steers, but you aren't human beings, get out of here, and fast, or I'll lay violent hands on you, don't hold me back, I know what I'm doing, I was in the dark too long.

Joan drives them out, using as a stick a flag held upside down. The Black Straw Hats appear in the doorways.

Get out! Are you trying to turn the house of God into a stable? Another Livestock Exchange? Get out! There's nothing for you here. We don't want to see such faces here. You're unworthy and I'm showing you the door. For all your money!

THE THREE: Very well. But forty months' rent goes with us – simply, modestly, irretrievably. We need every cent of it anyway: we're facing times as terrible as the livestock market has ever seen. *Exeunt.*

SNYDER, *running after them*: Please stay, gentlemen! Don't go, she has no authority at all! A crazy female! She'll be fired! She'll do whatever you want her to do.

JOAN, *to the Black Straw Hats*: Well, that certainly wasn't very smart at a time like this, what with the rent and all. But we can't think about that now. *To Luckerniddle and Gloomb*: Sit down back there, I'll bring you some soup.

SNYDER, *returning*:

Go on, make the poor your guests
And regale them with rainwater and fine speeches
When there's really no pity for them up above
Nothing but snow!
You followed your very first impulses
Utterly without humility! It is so much easier
Simply to drive the unclean out with arrogance.
You're squeamish about the bread we have to eat
Much too curious how it's made, and still
You want to eat it! Now, woman above the world
Get out in the rain and face the snowstorm in righteousness!

JOAN: Does that mean I'm to take off my uniform?

SNYDER: Take off your uniform and pack your bags! Get out of this house and take along the riff-raff you brought us. Nothing but riff-raff and scum followed you in here. Now you'll be in that class yourself. Go and get your things.

Joan goes out and comes back dressed like a country servant, carrying a little suitcase.

JOAN:

> I'll go find rich man Mauler, he is not
> Without fear or good will, and ask his help.
> I won't put on this coat or black straw hat
> Ever again or come back to this dear house
> Of songs and awakenings till
> I bring in rich man Mauler as one of us
> Converted from the ground up.
> What if their money has eaten away
> Their ears and human faces like a cancer
> Making them sit apart but loftily
> Beyond the reach of any cry for help!
> Poor cripples!
> There must be *one* just man among them!

Exit.

SNYDER:

> Poor simpleton!
> You're blind to this: set up in huge formations
> The givers and the takers of work
> Confront one another:
> Warring fronts: irreconcilable.
> Run to and fro between them, little peacemaker, little medi-
>   ator –
> Be useful to neither and go to your doom.

MULBERRY, *entering*: Have you the money now?

SNYDER: God will still be able to pay for the definitely scanty shelter He has found on earth, I said scanty, Mr Mulberry.

MULBERRY: Yes, pay, that's the ticket, that's the problem! You said the right word then, Snyder! If the Lord in His goodness pays, good. But if He doesn't pay, not so good. If the Lord in His goodness doesn't pay His rent, He'll have to get out, and what's more, He'll have to go on Saturday night, eh, Snyder?

Exit.

PIERPONT MAULER'S SPEECH ON THE INDISPENSABILITY OF CAPITALISM AND RELIGION

Mauler's Office

MAULER:

Well, Slift, today's the day
When our good friend Graham and all his crew
Who wanted to wait for the lowest livestock prices
Will have to buy the meat they owe us.

SLIFT:

It will cost them more, because anything
The Chicago market can show in the way of lowing cattle
Is ours now.
Every hog they owe us
They'll have to buy from us, and that's expensive.

MAULER:

Now, Slift, let loose all your wholesalers!
Let them torment the livestock market with demands
For everything that looks like hogs and cattle
And so make prices go up and up.

SLIFT:

What news of your Joan? There's a rumour
Around the Livestock Exchange that you slept with her.
I did my best to scotch it. She hasn't been heard of
Since that day she threw us all out of the temple:
It's as though black roaring Chicago had swallowed her up.

MAULER:

I liked her action very much
Throwing you all out like that. Yes, that girl's afraid of
   nothing.
And if I'd been along on that occasion
She'd have thrown me out with the rest and that's
What I like about her and that house of hers
The fact that people like me are impossible there.

Force the price up to eighty, Slift. That will make those
    Grahams
Rather like mud you stick your foot into
Merely to see its shape again.
I won't let an ounce of meat go by:
This time I'll rip their skins off for good and all
In accordance with my nature.

SLIFT:

I'm overjoyed that you've shaken off
Your weakness of the past few days. And now
I'll go and watch them buy up livestock.

MAULER:

It's high time this damn town had its skin ripped off
And those fellows were taught a thing or two
About the meat market: what if they do yell 'Crime!'

Enter Joan, carrying a suitcase.

JOAN: Good morning, Mr Mauler. You're a hard man to find.
I'll just leave my things over there for the time being. You
see, I'm not with the Black Straw Hats any more. We had an
argument. So I thought, well, I'll go and look after Mr
Mauler. Having no more of that wearing mission work to do,
I can pay more attention to the individual. So, to begin with,
I'm going to occupy myself with you a little, that is, if you'll
let me. You know, I've noticed that you are much more ap-
proachable than many other people. That's a fine old mohair
sofa you have there, but why do you have a sheet on it? –
and it isn't made up properly, either. So you sleep in your
office? I thought surely you would have one of those great
big palaces. *Mauler says nothing.* But you're quite right, Mr
Mauler, to be a good manager in little things too, being a
meat king. I don't know why, but when I see you I always
think of the story about the Lord when He visited Adam in
the Garden of Eden and called out, 'Adam, where are you?'
Do you remember? *She laughs.* Adam is standing behind a
bush with his arms up to the elbows in a doe, and he hears the
voice of God just like that, with blood all over him. And so

he acts as if he wasn't there. But God doesn't give up, and calls out again, 'Adam, where are you?' And then Adam says, faintly and blushing crimson: 'This is the time you pick to visit me, right after I've killed a doe. Oh, don't say a word, I know I shouldn't have done it.' But your conscience is clear, Mr Mauler, I hope.

MAULER: So you're not with the Black Straw Hats any more?

JOAN: No, Mr Mauler, and I don't belong there either.

MAULER: Then what have you been living on?

Joan says nothing.

I see. Nothing. How long ago did you leave the Black Straw Hats?

JOAN: Eight days ago.

MAULER, *turns away and weeps:*

So greatly changed, and in a mere eight days!

Where has she been? To whom has she been talking? What was it

That drew those lines around her mouth?

The city she has come from

Is a thing I do not yet know.

He brings her food on a tray.

I see you very much changed. Here's something to eat, if you like.

I'm not hungry myself.

JOAN, *looking at the food:* Mr Mauler, after we drove the rich people out of our house –

MAULER: Which amused me very much, and seemed the right thing to do –

JOAN: The landlord, who lives on the rent we pay, gave us notice to get out next Sunday.

MAULER: Indeed! So the Black Straw Hats are poorly off financially?

JOAN: Yes, and that's why I thought I'd go and see Mr Mauler.

She begins to eat hungrily.

MAULER: Don't you fret. I'll go into the market and get you the money you need. Yes, I'll do that, I'll get hold of it whatever it costs me, even if I have to slice it right out of the city's skin. I'll do it for you. Money's expensive, of course, but I'll produce it. That will be to your liking.

JOAN: Yes, Mr Mauler.

MAULER: So you go and tell them: 'The money is on the way. It will be there by Saturday. Mauler will get hold of it. He just left for the livestock market to dig it up.' That matter of the fifty thousand didn't go so well, not exactly as I wanted it. I was unable to get them work immediately. But for you I'll make an exception, and your Black Straw Hats shall be spared, I'll get the money for you. Run and tell them.

JOAN: Yes, Mr Mauler!

MAULER:

There, I've put it in writing. Take it.
I too am sorry that the men are waiting for work
In the stockyards and not very good work at that.
Fifty thousand men
Standing around in the stockyards, not even leaving at night.

Joan stops eating.

But that's the way this business goes:
It's to be or not to be – a question whether
I am to be the best man in my class or go
The dark and dreary way to the stockyards myself.
Also, the scum is filling up the yards again
And making trouble.
And now – I'll tell you the simple truth – I would have liked
To hear you say that what I do is right
And my business is natural: so
Tell me for sure that it was by your advice
I ordered meat from the meat-ring and from
The stockbreeders too, thus doing good; then
Because I know well that you are poor and right now
They're trying to take away the very roof over your heads
I'll give you something in return, as token
Of my goodwill.

JOAN: So the workers are still waiting in front of the slaughter-houses?

MAULER:

Why are you set against money? and yet look
So very different when you haven't any?
What do you think about money? Tell me
I want to know; and don't get wrong ideas
The way a fool will think of money as
Something to be doubted. Consider the reality
The plain truth, not pleasant maybe, but still
True for all that: everything is unsteady and the human race
Is exposed to luck, you might say, to the state of the weather
But money's a means of making some improvement – even if only
For certain people – apart from that, what a structure!
Built up from time immemorial, over and over again
Because it keeps collapsing, but still tremendous: demanding sacrifice
Very hard to set up, continually set up
With many a groan, but still inescapably
Wresting the possible from a reluctant planet
However much or little that may be; and accordingly defended
At all times by the best. Just think, if I –
Who have much against it, and sleep badly –
Were to desert it, I would be like a fly
Ceasing to hold back a landslide. There and then
I would become a nothing and it would keep on going over me.
For otherwise everything would have to be overturned
And the architect's design fundamentally altered
To suit an utterly different, incredible, new valuation of man
Which you people don't want any more than we do, for it would take effect
With neither us nor God, who would have no function left
And be dismissed accordingly. Therefore you really ought to
Collaborate with us, and even if you don't sacrifice

What we don't want of you anyhow, still sanction the sacri-
fices:
In a word, you really ought
To set God up once more –
The only salvation – and
Beat the drum for Him so that He may
Gain a foothold in the regions of misery and His
Voice may ring out over the stockyards.
That would suffice.

Holding out the note to her.

Take what you get, but know the reason
Before you take it! Here's the voucher, this is four years' rent.

JOAN:

Mr Mauler, I don't understand what you have been saying
And do not wish to either.

Rising.

I know I should be overjoyed to hear
That God is going to be helped, only
I belong to those for whom
This does not mean real help. And to whom
Nothing is offered.

MAULER:

If you take the money to the Black Straw Hats you can also
Stay in their house again: this living
On nothing is not good for you. Believe me
They're out for money, and so they should be.

JOAN:

If the Black Straw Hats
Accept your money they are welcome to it
But I will take my stand among the people waiting in the
stockyards
Until the factories open up again, and
Eat nothing but what they eat and if
They are offered snow, then snow
And the work they do I will do also, for I have no money
either

63

And no other way to get it – honourably, anyhow –
And if there is no more work, then let there be none
For me either, and
You, who live on poverty and
Cannot bear to see the poor and judge
Something you do not know and make arrangements
So as not to see what sits there being judged
Abandoned in the stockyards, disregarded
If you want to see me again
Come to the stockyards.

Exit.

MAULER:

Tonight then, Mauler
Get up every hour and look out of the window
To see if it's snowing, and if it is
It will be snowing on the girl you know.

9

JOAN'S THIRD DESCENT INTO THE DEPTHS: THE SNOWFALL

a

Stockyards District

JOAN:

Listen to the dream I had one night
A week ago.
Before me in a little field, too small
To hold the shade of a middle-sized tree, hemmed in
By enormous houses, I saw a bunch
Of people: I could not make out how many, but
There were far more of them than all the sparrows
That could find room in such a tiny place –
A very thick bunch indeed, so that
The field began to buckle and rise in the middle
And the bunch was suspended on its edge, holding fast

A moment, quivering: then, stirred
By the intervention of a word – uttered somewhere or other
Meaning nothing vital – it began to flow.
Then I saw processions, streets, familiar ones, Chicago! You!
I saw you marching, then I saw myself:
I, silent, saw myself striding at your head
With warlike step and bloodstains on my brow
And shouting words that sounded militant
In a tongue I did not know; and while many processions
Moved in many directions all at once
I strode in front of many processions in manifold shapes:
Young and old, sobbing and cursing
Finally beside myself! Virtue and terror!
Changing whatever my foot touched
Causing measureless destruction, visibly influencing
The courses of the stars, but also changing utterly
The neighbourhood streets familiar to us all.
So the procession moved, and I along with it
Veiled by snow from any hostile attack
Transparent with hunger, no target
Not to be hit anywhere, not being settled anywhere;
Not to be touched by any trouble, being accustomed
To all. And so it marches, abandoning the position
Which cannot be held: exchanging it for any other one.
That was my dream.
Today I see its meaning:
Before tomorrow morning we
Will start out from these yards
And reach their city, Chicago, in the gray of dawn
Displaying the full range of our wretchedness in public places
Appealing to whatever resembles a human being.
What will come after, I do not know.

GLOOMB: Did you understand that, Mrs Luckerniddle? I didn't.

MRS LUCKERNIDDLE: If she hadn't talked so big to the Black
    Straw Hats we'd be sitting where it's warm now, and spoon-
    ing up our soup!

b

Livestock Exchange

MAULER, *to the packers*:

My friends in New York have written me to say
That the tariff in the south
Was repealed today.

THE PACKERS:

This is awful, the tariff law gone and here we are
Without any meat to sell! It's been sold already
At a low price and now we are asked to buy meat when it's
    going up!

THE STOCKBREEDERS:

This is awful, the tariff law gone and here we are
Without any livestock to sell! It's already been sold
At a lower price!

THE SMALL SPECULATORS:

Awful! Eternally inscrutable
Are the eternal laws
Of human economy!
Without warning
The volcano erupts and lays the country waste!
Without an invitation
The profitable island rises from the barren seas!
No one is told, no one is in the picture! But the last in line
Is bitten by the dogs!

MAULER: Well, seeing that livestock is being demanded
In cans at an acceptable price
I now request you to hand over quickly
The canned meat I am supposed to get from you
According to contract.

GRAHAM: At the old price?

MAULER:

As the contract specified, Graham.
Four hundred tons, if I remember correctly
A moment when I was not myself.

THE PACKERS:

> How can we take livestock now, with prices rising?
> Someone has made a corner in it
> Nobody knows who –
> Release us from the contract, Mauler!

MAULER:

> Unfortunately I must have those cans. But there is
> Still livestock enough, a bit expensive, granted, but
> Livestock enough. Buy it up!

THE PACKERS: Buy livestock now? The hell with it!

c

A little Tavern in the Stockyards District

Men and women workers, Joan among them. – A group of Black Straw Hats enter. Joan rises and makes frantic gestures at them during what follows.

JACKSON, *a Black Straw Hat lieutenant, after a hurried song*:

> Brother, why won't you eat the bread that Jesus gives?
> See how happy and glad are we.
> It's because we have found the Lord Jesus, Lord of all our lives.
> Hurry, come to Him heartily!
> Hallelujah!

One of the Black Straw Hat girls talks to the workers, making side remarks to her comrades.

MARTHA, *a Black Straw Hat private*: (It's no use, is it?) Brothers and sisters, I too used to stand sadly by the wayside, just as you are, and the old Adam in me cared for nothing but meat and drink, but then I found my Lord Jesus, and then it was so light and glad inside me, but now (They aren't listening at all!) if I just think real hard about my Lord Jesus, who redeemed us all by His suffering in spite of our many wicked deeds, then I stop feeling hungry and thirsty, except for our Lord Jesus' word. (No use.) Where the Lord Jesus is, there is not violence, but peace, not hate but love. (It's quite hopeless!)

THE BLACK STRAW HATS: Hallelujah!

Jackson passes the box around. Nothing is put into it.

Hallelujah!

JOAN:
If only they wouldn't stay here in the cold
Making all that nuisance and talking, talking!
Really, now I can hardly bear
To hear the words
That once were dear and pleasant to me! If only a voice
Some remnant inside them, would say:
There's snow and wind here, be quiet here!

A WOMAN: Oh, let them be. They have to do this to get a bit of warmth and food. I wish I was in their shoes.

MRS LUCKERNIDDLE: That was nice music!

GLOOMB: Nice and short.

MRS LUCKERNIDDLE: But they really are good people.

GLOOMB: Good and brief, short and sweet.

A WOMAN WORKER: Why don't they give us a real talk, and convert us?

GLOOMB, *making a gesture of paying out money*: Can you keep the pot boiling, Mrs Swingurn?

THE WOMAN WORKER: The music is very pretty but I was expecting them to give us a plate of soup, maybe, seeing they had brought a pot along.

A WORKER, *surprised at her*: No kidding, you thought that?

MRS LUCKERNIDDLE: I'd rather see some action, too. I've heard enough speeches. If certain people had kept quiet, I'd have a place to lay my head tonight.

JOAN: Are there no people here with any enterprise?

THE WORKER: Yes, the Communists.

JOAN: Aren't they people who incite to crime?

THE WORKER: No.

A silence.

JOAN: Where are they?

GLOOMB: Mrs Luckerniddle can tell you.

JOAN, *to Mrs Luckerniddle*: How do you happen to know?

MRS LUCKERNIDDLE: I'll tell you. In days gone by, before I started counting on people like you, I went there often, because of my husband.

d

Livestock Exchange

THE PACKERS:

We're buying livestock! Yearlings!

Feeders! Calves! Steers! Hogs!

Offers, please!

THE STOCKBREEDERS: There isn't any! We've sold whatever was saleable.

THE PACKERS: Isn't any? The depots are bursting with cattle.

THE STOCKBREEDERS: Sold.

THE PACKERS: To whom?

Enter Mauler.

The packers mill around him.

Not a steer to be found in Chicago!

You'll have to give us more time, Mauler.

MAULER: You'll deliver your meat as agreed.

Going over to Slift.

Squeeze 'em dry.

A STOCKBREEDER: Eight hundred Kentucky steers at four hundred.

THE PACKERS: Impossible. Four hundred! Are you crazy?

SLIFT: I'll take them. At four hundred.

THE STOCKBREEDERS: Eight hundred steers sold to Sullivan Slift for four hundred.

THE PACKERS:

It's Mauler! What did we say? He's the one!

You crooked hound! He makes us deliver canned meat

And buys up livestock! So we have to buy from him
The meat we need to fill his cans!
You filthy butcher! Here, take *our* flesh, hack yourself off
  a slice!

MAULER: If you're a dumb ox you shouldn't be surprised when
  people's appetites grow with looking at you.

GRAHAM *makes as if to attack Mauler*: He's got it coming, I'll
  settle his hash!

MAULER:

All right, Graham, now I demand your cans.
You can stuff yourself into one of them.
I'll teach you the meat business, you
Traders! From now on I get paid, and well paid
For every hoof, every calf from here to Illinois*
And so I'll offer five hundred steers at fifty-six to start with.

Dead silence.

And now, in view of the weak demand, seeing nobody here
  needs livestock
I demand sixty! And don't forget my cans, either!

e

Another part of the Stockyards

*Placards are inscribed: Solidarity with Locked-out Stockyard
Workers! All out for General Strike! In front of a shed two men
from the union local are speaking to a group of workers. Enter Joan.*

JOAN: Are these the people who lead the movement of the unemployed? I can help them. I've learned to speak in streets
  and meeting-halls, I have no fear of hecklers and I think I
  can explain a good thing well. Because, as I see it, something's
  got to be done right away. I have some suggestions to make,
  too.

A LABOUR LEADER: Listen, all. So far the meat gang hasn't
  shown the least inclination to open up its factories. At first it

Sic.–F.J.

seemed that the exploiter Pierpont Mauler was all out for a reopening because he wants from the meat gang huge quantities of meat that they owe him by contract. Then it became clear that the meat they need for packing is in Mauler's own hands and he won't even consider letting it go. Now we know that if things are left up to the meat gang we workers will never all get back into the slaughter-houses, and never at the old wages. With things in this pass we've got to realize that nothing can help us but the use of force. The city utilities have promised to join the general strike by tomorrow morning at the latest. Now this news must be spread in all parts of the stockyards; if it isn't, there's a danger that the masses will be excited by some rumour or other and leave the yards, and then be forced to yield to the meat gang's terms. So these letters, stating that the gas works and water works and power stations are going to help us by going on strike, must be handed out to delegates who will be awaiting our password in different parts of the stockyards at ten o'clock tonight. Stick that under your vest, Jack, and wait for the delegates in front of Mother Schmitt's canteen.

A worker takes the letter and leaves.

SECOND WORKER: Give me the one for the Graham works, I know them.

THE LEADER: 26th Street, corner Michigan Park.

The worker takes the letter and leaves.

13th Street by the Westinghouse Building. *To Joan*: Well, and who may you be?

JOAN: I was fired from the job I had.

THE LEADER: What job?

JOAN: Selling magazines.

THE LEADER: Who were you working for?

JOAN: I'm a peddler.

A WORKER: Maybe she's a spy.

THE LABOUR LEADER: No, I know her, she's with the Salvation Army, and well known to the police. Nobody would suspect her of working for us. That's in our favour, because the cops are on a sharp lookout at the place the comrades from the Cridle plant are making for. None of our people could pass in a crowd the way she could.

THE OTHER LEADER: Who can tell what she will do with the letter we give her?

FIRST LEADER: Nobody.

To Joan.

A net with a torn mesh
Is of no use:
The fish swim through at that spot
As though there were no net.
Suddenly all its meshes
Are useless.

JOAN: I used to sell papers on 44th Street. I'm no spy. I'm for your cause heart and soul.

SECOND LEADER: Our cause? Why, isn't it your cause?

JOAN: It certainly isn't in the public interest for the factory owners to leave all those people sitting in the streets just like that. Why, it makes you think the poverty of the poor is useful to the rich! You might say poverty is all their doing! *The workers laugh uproariously.* It's inhuman, that's what it is! I even have people like Mauler in mind when I say that. *Renewed laughter.* Why do you laugh? I don't think you have any right to be malicious and to believe without proof that a man like Mauler can be inhuman.

SECOND LEADER: Not without proof! You can give the letter to her, all right. You know her, Mrs Luckerniddle? *Mrs Luckerniddle nods.* She's honest, isn't she?

MRS LUCKERNIDDLE: She's honest, all right.

FIRST LEADER: Go to Storehouse Five at the Graham plant. When you see three workers come up and look around them, ask if they are from the Cridle plant. This letter is for them.

72

f

Livestock Exchange

THE SMALL SPECULATORS:

Quotations going down! The packing plants in peril!
What will become of us, the stockholders?
The man with small savings who gave his last cent
For the middle class, which is weakened anyway?
A man like Graham ought to be
Torn to shreds before he makes waste paper
Out of the note with our share marked on it, the one
We earned from his bloody cellars.
Buy that livestock, buy it at any price!

*Throughout this scene the names of firms suspending payment are
being called out. 'Suspending payment: Meyer & Co.', etc.*

THE PACKERS: We can do no more, the price is over seventy.

THE WHOLESALERS: Mow 'em down, they won't buy, the high-
hats.

THE PACKERS: Two thousand steers demanded at seventy.

SLIFT, *to Mauler, beside a column*: Shove 'em up.

MAULER:

I see that you have not stood by your part
Of the contract I drew up with you that day
In the wish to create employment. And now I hear
They're still standing around out there in the yards. But
You're going to regret it: out with the canned meat
Which I have bought!

GRAHAM:

There's nothing we can do: meat has completely
Vanished from the market!
I'll take five hundred steers at seventy-five.

THE SMALL SPECULATORS:

Buy them, you greedy hounds!
They won't buy! They'd rather hand over
The packing plants.

MAULER:

> We shouldn't push it any higher, Slift.
> They're powerless now.
> They are meant to bleed, but they mustn't perish;
> If they go out we're goners too.

SLIFT:

> There's life in them yet, put it up a notch.
> Five hundred steers at seventy-seven.

THE SMALL SPECULATORS:

> Did you hear that? Why
> Didn't they buy at seventy-five? Now
> It's gone to seventy-seven and still climbing.

THE PACKERS: We get fifty from Mauler for the cans and can't pay Mauler eighty for the livestock.

MAULER, *to a group of men*: Where are the people I sent to the stockyards?

A MAN: There's one.

MAULER: Well, let's have it.

The first detective reports.

FIRST DETECTIVE: Those crowds, Mr Mauler, you can't see the end of them. If you called the name of Joan, ten or maybe a hundred would answer. The mob sits there and waits, without a face or a name. Besides, nobody can hear just one man's voice and there are far too many people running around asking after relatives they've lost. Serious unrest prevails in the sections where the unions are at work.

MAULER: Who's at work? The unions? And the police let them agitate? Damn it all! Go and call the police right away, mention my name, ask them what we're paying taxes for. Insist that the troublemakers get their heads cracked, speak plainly to them.

Exit first detective.

GRAHAM:

> Oh, give us a thousand at seventy-seven, Mauler;
> If it knocks us out, it's the end of us.

SLIFT: Five hundred to Graham at seventy-seven. All the rest
at eighty.

MAULER, *returning*:

Slift, this business no longer entertains me.

It might take us too far.

Go up to eighty, then let it go at eighty.

I'll hand it over and let them go.

Enough's enough. The town needs a breathing-spell.

And I have other worries.

Slift, this throat-squeezing isn't as much fun

As I thought it would be.

Seeing the second detective.

Did you find her?

SECOND DETECTIVE: No, I saw no woman in a Black Straw Hat
uniform. There are a hundred thousand people standing
around in the stockyards; besides, it's dark, and that biting
wind drowns your voice. Also, the police are clearing the
yards and shots are being fired already.

MAULER:

Shots? At whom? Oh, yes, of course.

It seems strange – you can't hear a thing in this place.

So she's not to be found, and shots are being fired?

Go to the phone-booth, look for Jim and tell him

Not to call, or people will say again

That we demanded the shooting.

Exit second detective.

MEYERS: Fifteen hundred at eighty!

SLIFT: Not more than five hundred at eighty!

MEYERS: Five hundred at eighty, you cutthroat!

MAULER, *returning to the column*: Slift, I feel unwell. Let up,
will you?

SLIFT: I wouldn't think of it. There's life in them yet. And if
you start to weaken, Mauler, I'll shove them up higher.

MAULER:

Slift, I need a breath of air. You carry on

The business. I can't. Carry it on

The way I would. I'd rather give it all away
Than have more things happen because of me!
Go no higher than eighty-five! But manage it
The way I would. You know me.

Exit. On his way out he meets reporters.

THE REPORTERS: What's new, Mauler?

MAULER, *departing*: It must be announced in the stockyards that
I have now sold livestock to the slaughterhouses, at cost, so
livestock's available now. Otherwise, there will be violence.

SLIFT: Five hundred steers at ninety!

THE SMALL SPECULATORS:
We heard that Mauler was willing
To sell at eighty-five. Slift has no authority.

SLIFT:
That's a lie! I'll teach you
To sell meat in cans and then
Not to have any meat!
Five thousand steers for ninety-five!

Uproar.

g
Stockyards

Many people waiting, Joan among them.

PEOPLE: Why are you sitting here?

JOAN: I have to deliver a letter. Three men are supposed to come
by here.

A group of reporters comes up, led by a man.

THE MAN, *pointing to Joan*: That's the one. *To Joan*: These
people are reporters.

THE REPORTERS: Hello, are you Joan Dark, the Black Straw
Hat?

JOAN: No.

THE REPORTERS: We have heard from Mauler's office that you've
sworn not to leave the stockyards before the plants open up.

We have it, you can read it here, in big front-page headlines.
Joan turns away. Our Lady of the Stockyards Avers God
Solidly Behind Stockyard Workers.

JOAN: I said no such thing.

THE REPORTERS: We can assure you, Miss Dark, that public
opinion is on your side. All Chicago sympathizes with you,
except a few unscrupulous speculators. Your Black Straw
Hats will reap terrific success from all this.

JOAN: I'm not with the Black Straw Hats any more.

THE REPORTERS: That can't be. For us, you belong to the Black
Straw Hats. But we don't want to disturb you, we'll keep
well in the background.

JOAN: I would like you to go away.

They sit down some distance off.

THE WORKERS, *in the stockyards, rear*:
Before our need is at its worst
They will not open the factories.
When misery has mounted
They will open up.
But they must answer us.
Do not go, wait for the answer.

COUNTER-CHORUS, *also rear*:
Wrong! Let misery mount
They will not open up!
Not before their profits rise.
Their answer will come
From cannon and machine-guns.
The only help we have is from ourselves
Our only call can be
To people like us.

JOAN: Do you think so too, Mrs Luckerniddle?

MRS LUCKERNIDDLE: Yes, that's the truth.

JOAN:
I see this system and on the surface
It has long been familiar to me, but not
In its inner meaning! Some, a few, sit up above

And many down below and the ones on top
Shout down: 'Come on up, then we'll all
Be on top', but if you look closely you'll see
Something hidden between the ones on top and the ones below
That looks like a path but is not a path –
It's a plank and now you can see it quite clearly
It is a seesaw, this whole system
Is a seesaw, with two ends that depend
On one another, and those on top
Sit up there only because the others sit below
And only as long as they sit below;
They'd no longer be on top if the others came up
Leaving their place, so that of course
They want the others to sit down there
For all eternity and never come up.
Besides, there have to be more below than above
Or else the seesaw wouldn't hold. A seesaw, that's what it is.

The reporters get up and move upstage, having received some news.

A WORKER, *to Joan*: Say, what have you to do with those fellows?
JOAN: Nothing.
THE WORKER: But they were talking with you.
JOAN: They took me for someone else.
AN OLD MAN, *to Joan*: You sure look frozen. Like a swig of whisky? *Joan drinks.* Stop! Stop! That's no mean shot you took!
A WOMAN: Scandalous!
JOAN: Did you say something?
WOMAN: I said, scandalous! Guzzling all the old man's whisky!
JOAN: Shut your trap, you silly old thing. Hey, where's my shawl? They've gone and swiped it again. That's the last straw! Going and stealing my shawl, on top of everything else! Now who's got my shawl? Give it here pronto.

She grabs a sack off the head of the woman standing next to her. The woman resists.

Oh, so it's you. No lies! Gimme that sack.
THE WOMAN: Help, she's killing me!

A MAN: Shut up!

Someone throws her a rag.

JOAN:

    For all you people care, I might be sitting around in this
draft nekkid.
It wasn't as cold as this in my dream.
When I came to this place with brave plans
Fortified by dreams, I still never dreamed
That it could be so cold here. Now the only thing I miss
Of all I have is my nice warm shawl.
You may well be hungry, you have nothing to eat
But they're waiting for me with a bowl of soup.
You may well freeze
But I can go into the warm hall any time
Pick up the flag and beat the drum
And speak about HIM who lives in the clouds. After all
What did you leave? What I left
Was no mere calling, though it was a noble
Profession, but a decent job as well
And daily bread and a roof and a livelihood.
Yes, it seems almost like a play
Something undignified, for me to stay in this place
Without extremely pressing need. And yet
I may not go, and still –
I'll be frank about it – fear tightens round my throat
At the thought of this not eating, not sleeping, not knowing
    where you are
Habitual hunger, helpless cold and –
Worst of all – wanting to get away.

THE WORKERS:

    Stay here! Whatever happens,
Do not break ranks!
Only if you stand together
Can you help each other!
Realize that you have been betrayed
By all your public sponsors

And your unions, which are bought.
Listen to no one, believe nothing
But test every proposal
That leads to genuine change. And above all learn:
It will only work out by force
And only if you do it yourselves.

The reporters return.

THE REPORTERS: Hey there, gal, you've had sensational success: we've just found out that the millionaire Pierpont Mauler, who has vast quantities of livestock in his hands now, is releasing it to the slaughter-houses in spite of rising prices. This being so, work will be resumed in the yards tomorrow.

JOAN: Oh, what good news!

MRS LUCKERNIDDLE: Those are the lies our people spoke of. It's a good thing the truth is in our letter.

JOAN:

Listen, there's work to be had!
The ice has thawed in their hearts. At least
The one just man among them
Has not failed us. Appealed to as a man
He has answered as a man.
There *is* kindness in the world.

Machine guns rat-a-tat in the distance.

What's that noise?

A REPORTER: Those are army machine guns. The army has orders to clear the stockyards because the agitators who are inciting to violence will have to be silenced now that the slaughterhouses are to be reopened.

A WOMAN: Shall we go home now?

A WORKER: How do we know if it's true that jobs are to be had again?

JOAN: Why shouldn't it be true, if these gentlemen say so? People don't joke about things like that.

MRS LUCKERNIDDLE: Don't talk such foolishness. You have no sense at all. It's because you haven't been sitting out here in the cold long enough. *She gets up.* I'll run over to our people

now, and tell them the lying has started. And listen: don't
you stir from here with that letter!

JOAN: But there's shooting going on.

A WORKER: You just take it easy and stay here. The stockyards
are so big it'll take the army hours to get this far.

JOAN: How many people are there in them now, anyway?

A REPORTER: There must be a hundred thousand.

JOAN:

So many?

Oh, what an unknown school, an unlawful space

Filled up with snow, where hunger is teacher and unpre-
ventably

Need speaks about necessity.

A hundred thousand pupils, what are you learning?

THE WORKERS, *rear*:

If you stay together

They will cut you to pieces.

We advise you to stay together!

If you fight

Their tanks will grind you to pulp.

We advise you to fight!

This battle will be lost

And maybe the next

Will also be lost.

But you are learning to fight

And realizing

That it will only work out by force

And only if you do it yourselves.

JOAN:

Stop: no more lessons

So coldly learned!

Do not use force

To fight disorder and confusion.

Certainly the temptation is tremendous!

Another night like this, another wordless

Oppression like this, and nobody

Will be able to keep quiet. And certainly

You have already stood together
On many a night in many a year and learned
To think coldly and terribly.
Certainly acts of violence and weakness
Are matching one another in the dark
And unsettled business is piling up.
But the meal that's cooking here – who
Will be the ones to eat it?
I'm leaving. What's done by force cannot be good. I don't
belong with them. If hunger and the tread of misery had
taught me violence as a child, I would belong to them and
ask no questions. But as it is, I must leave.

She remains seated.

THE REPORTERS: Our advice to you is, leave the stockyards right
now. You made a big hit, but that's over and done with.

Exeunt. Shouting, rear, spreading forward. The workers rise.

A WORKER: They're bringing the men from the local. *The two
leaders of the workers are brought forward, handcuffed.*
A WORKER, *to his handcuffed leader*: Never mind, William, it
isn't evening every day.
ANOTHER, *shouting after the group*: Bloodhounds!
THE WORKERS: If they think they're stopping anything that way,
they're on the wrong track. Our men have taken care of
everything.

In a vision Joan sees herself as a criminal, outside the familiar world.

JOAN:
The men who gave me the letter! Why are they
Handcuffed? What is in the letter?
I could do nothing
That would have to be done by force and
Would provoke force. A person like that would stand
Against his fellow man, full of malice
And beyond the range of any settlement
That human beings usually make.

Not belonging, he would lose his way
In a world no longer familiar to him. The stars
Would hurtle past his head breaking
The ancient rules. Words
Would change meaning for him. Innocence
Would abandon one who was constantly persecuted.
He can look at nothing without suspicion.
I could not be like that. So I'm leaving.
For three days Joan was seen
In Packingtown, in the stockyard swamps
Going down, downward from level to level
To clear the mud away, to manifest
To the lowest. Three days walking
Down the slope, growing weaker on the third
And finally swallowed by the swamp. Say:
'It was too cold.'

She gets up and goes. Snow begins to fall.

MRS LUCKERNIDDLE: All lies. Say, what's become of the person
  that was sitting beside me?

A WOMAN: Gone.

A WORKER: I thought right away that she'd take off when the
  real snow came.

*Three workers come by, look around for someone, fail to find him,
and leave. As it grows dark, a writing appears:*

The snow is starting to fall
Will anyone stay at all?
They'll stay today as they've stayed before –
Stony ground and folk that are poor.

h

PIERPONT MAULER CROSSES THE BOUNDARY OF POVERTY

A Chicago Street Corner

MAULER, *to one of the detectives*:

No further, let's turn back now, what do you say?
Admit it: you laughed. I said, 'Let's turn back now'
And you laughed. They're shooting again.
Seems to be some resistance, eh? But this is what
I wanted to impress upon you: think nothing of it
If I turned back a couple of times
As we came nearer the stockyards. Thinking
Is nothing. I'm not paying you to think.
I probably have my reasons. I'm known down there.
Now you are thinking again. Seems I've taken
A couple of nitwits along. Anyway
Let's turn back. I hope the person I was looking for
Has listened to reason and left that place
Where hell appears to be breaking loose.

A newsboy goes by.

Aha! the papers! let's see how the livestock market is going!

He reads, and turns pale.

Well, something's happened here that changes things:
It's printed here, black on white, that livestock
Is down to thirty and not a slice is being sold
That's what it says here, black on white, the packers
Are ruined and have left the livestock market.
And it also says that Mauler and Slift, his friend
Are the worst hit of all. That's what it says and it means
That things have reached a point that certainly was not
    striven for
But is greeted with sighs of relief. I can help them no further –
I freely offered
All my livestock for the use of any man that wanted it
And nobody took it and so I am free now

84

And without pretensions and hereby
I dismiss you in order to cross
The boundary of poverty, for I no longer require your ser-
    vices.
Henceforth nobody will want to knock me down.

THE TWO DETECTIVES: Then we may go.

MAULER:

You may indeed, and so may I, wherever I want.
Even to the stockyards.
And as for the thing made of sweat and money
Which we have erected in these cities:
It already seems as though a man
Had made a building, the largest in the world and
The most expensive and practical, but –
By an oversight, and because it was cheap – he used dog-shit
As its material, so that it would have been very difficult
To live in and in the end his only glory was
That he had made the biggest stink in the world.
And anyone who gets out of a building like that
Should be a cheerful man.

A DETECTIVE, *departing*: So, he's finished.

MAULER:

Bad luck may crush the man of humble size;
Me it must waft to spiritual skies.

i

A deserted section of the Stockyards

In the blizzard Mrs. Luckerniddle meets Joan.

MRS LUCKERNIDDLE: There you are! Where are you off to?
Have you delivered the letter?

JOAN: No. I'm leaving this place.

MRS LUCKERNIDDLE: I thought as much. Give me the letter,
right now!

JOAN: No, you won't get it. You don't have to come any closer.
There's just more incitement to violence in it, that's all.
Everything's all right now, but you want to keep on.

MRS LUCKERNIDDLE: So you think everything's all right! And I said you were honest – or else they wouldn't have given you the letter in the first place. But you're a crook – you're with the others. Scum, that's what you are! Hand over the letter they entrusted to you! *Joan vanishes in the blizzard.* Hey, you! She's gone again.

j

Another part of the City

Joan, hurrying towards the city, overhears two passing workers.

FIRST WORKER: First they let the rumour leak out that work would start up again, full blast, in the stockyards; but now that a part of the workers have left the yards to come back early tomorrow morning, they're suddenly saying that the slaughterhouses won't be opened at all, because Mauler has ruined them.

SECOND WORKER: The Communists were right. The masses shouldn't have broken ranks. All the more so because the Chicago utilities had all called a general strike for tomorrow.

FIRST WORKER: We didn't know that.

SECOND WORKER: That's bad. Some of the messengers must have failed us. A lot of people would have stayed put if they'd known about it. Even in the teeth of the cops' violence.

Wandering to and fro, Joan hears voices.

A VOICE:
He who does not arrive
Can plead no excuse. The fallen man
Is not excused by the stone.
Let not even the one who does arrive
Bore us with reports of difficulties
But deliver in silence
Himself or what is entrusted to him.

Joan has stood still and now runs in another direction.

A VOICE, *Joan stands still*:
> We gave you orders
> Our situation was critical
> We did not know who you were
> You might carry out our orders and you might
> Also betray us.
> Did you carry them out?

Joan runs farther and is halted by another voice.

A VOICE: Where men are waiting, someone must arrive!

Looking around for an escape from the voices, Joan hears voices on all sides.

VOICES:
> The net with a torn mesh
> Is of no use:
> The fish swim through it at that point
> As though there were no net.
> Suddenly all its meshes
> Are useless.

VOICE OF MRS LUCKERNIDDLE:
> I vouched for you.
> But the letter that contained the truth
> You did not deliver.

Joan falls to her knees.

JOAN:
> Oh, truth, shining light! Darkened by a snowstorm in an evil
> hour!
> Lost to sight from that moment! Oh, how violent are snow-
> storms!
> Oh, weakness of the flesh! What do you let live, hunger?
> What can outlast you, frost of the night?
> I must turn back!

She runs back.

10

PIERPONT MAULER HUMBLES HIMSELF AND IS EXALTED

The Black Straw Hats' Mission

MARTHA, *to another Black Straw Hat*: Three days ago a messenger from Pierpont Mauler, the meat king, came to tell us that he wishes to pay our rent and join us in a big campaign for the poor.

MULBERRY: Mr Snyder, it's Saturday evening. I'm asking you to pay your rent, which is very low, or get out of my building.

SNYDER: Mr Mulberry, we expect Mr Pierpont Mauler any minute now and he has promised us his support.

MULBERRY: Dick, old man, Albert, old man, put the furniture out in the street.

Two men begin to move the furniture out.

THE BLACK STRAW HATS:
Oh! They're taking the prayer bench!
Their greedy grasp even threatens
Pipe organ and pulpit.
And louder still we cry:
Please, rich Mr Mauler, come
And save us with your money!

SNYDER: Seven days now the masses have been standing
In rusting stockyards, cut off from work at last.
Freed from every kind of shelter they stand
Under rain and snow again, sensing above them
The zenith of an unknown decision.
Oh, dear Mr Mulberry, give us hot soup now
And a little music and they'll be ours. In my head I see
The Kingdom of Heaven ready and waiting.
Just give us a band and some decent soup
Really nourishing, and God will settle things
And all of Bolshevism, too
Will have breathed its last.

THE BLACK STRAW HATS:

The dams of faith have burst
In this Chicago of ours
And the slimy flood of materialism surges
Menacingly round the last of its houses.
Look, it's tottering, look, it's sinking!
Never mind – keep going – rich man Mauler's on the way!
He's started out already with all his money!

A BLACK STRAW HAT: Where can we put the public now, Major?

Enter three poor people, Mauler among them.

SNYDER, *shouting at them*: Soup, that's all you want! No soup
here! Just the Word of God! We'll get rid of them straight
off when they hear that.

MAULER: Here are three men coming to their God.

SNYDER: Sit down over there and keep quiet.

The three sit down. A man enters.

THE MAN: Is Pierpont Mauler here?

SNYDER: No, but we're expecting him.

THE MAN: The packers want to speak to him, and the stockbreeders are screaming for him.

Exit.

MAULER, *facing the audience*:

I hear they're looking for a man named Mauler.
I knew him: a numskull. Now they're searching
High and low, in heaven and hell
For that man Mauler who was dumber all his life
Than a dirty drink-sodden tramp.

Rises and goes over to the Black Straw Hats.

I knew a man who once was asked
For a hundred dollars. And he had about ten million.
And he came along without the hundred but threw
The ten million away
And gave himself.

He takes two of the Black Straw Hats and kneels with them on the prayer bench.

> I wish to confess my sins.
> No one who ever knelt here, friends
> Was as humble as I am.

THE BLACK STRAW HATS:

> Don't lose confidence
> Don't be souls of little faith!
> He's sure to come – already he's approaching
> With all his money.

A BLACK STRAW HAT: Is he here yet?

MAULER:

> A hymn, I pray you! For my heart
> Feels heavy and light at once.

TWO MUSICIANS: One piece, but no more.

They intone a hymn. The Black Straw Hats join in abstractedly, eyes on the door.

SNYDER, *bent over the account books*:

> I won't tell how this comes out.
> Quiet!
> Bring me the housekeeping record and the unpaid bills. I've
>   got to that stage.

MAULER:

> I accuse myself of exploitation
> Misuse of power, expropriation of everybody
> In the name of property. For seven days I held
> The city of Chicago by the throat
> Until it perished.

A BLACK STRAW HAT: That's Mauler!

MAULER:

> But at the same time I plead that on the seventh day
> I rid myself of everything, so that now
> I stand before you without possessions.
> Not guiltless, but repentant.

SNYDER: Are you Mauler?

MAULER: Yes; and torn to pieces by remorse.

SNYDER, *with a loud cry*: And without any money? *To the Black Straw Hats*: Pack up the stuff, I hereby suspend all payments.

THE MUSICIANS:
If that's the man you were waiting for
To get the cash to pay us with
Then we can go. Good night.

Exeunt.

CHORUS OF BLACK STRAW HATS, *gazing after the departing musicians*:
We were awaiting with prayers
The wealthy Mauler, but into our house
Came the man converted.
His heart
He brought to us, but not his money.
Therefore our hearts are moved, but
Our faces are long.

Confusedly the Black Straw Hats sing their last hymns as they sit on their last chairs and benches.

By the waters of Lake Michigan
We sit down and weep.
Take the proverbs off the walls
Shove the songbooks into the cloth that wraps the defeated
flag
For we can pay our bills no more
And against us rush the snowstorms
Of approaching winter.

Then they sing 'Go into the Thick of the Fight'. Mauler joins in, looking over a Black Straw Hat's shoulder.

SNYDER:
Quiet! Everybody out now – *to Mauler* – especially you!
Where is the forty months' rent from the unconverted
Whom Joan expelled? Look what she's driven in instead!
Oh, Joan
Give me my forty months' rent again!

MAULER:

> I see you would like to build your house
> In my shade. Well, for you a man
> Is what can help you; likewise, for me
> A man was only plunder. But even
> If man were only what is helped
> There would be no difference. Then you'd need drowning men
> For then it would be your business
> To be straws for them to clutch at. So all remains
> Within the mighty orbit of wares, like that of the stars.
> Such teaching, Snyder, leaves many souls embittered.
> But I can see that as I am
> I'm the wrong man for you.

Mauler makes to go, but the meat kings stop him at the door; they are all white as chalk.

THE PACKERS:

> Forgive us, noble Mauler, for seeking you out
> Disturbing you amid the involved emotions
> Of your colossal head.
> For we are ruined. Chaos is around us
> And over us the zenith of an unknown intention.
> What are you planning for us, Mauler?
> What will your next step be? We're sensitive
> To the blows you rain on our necks.

Enter the stockbreeders in great commotion, equally pale.

THE STOCKBREEDERS:

> Damnable Mauler, is this where you've sneaked off to?
> You pay for our livestock, instead of getting converted!
> Your money, not your soul! You would not need
> To lighten your conscience in a place like this
> If you hadn't lightened our pockets! Pay for our livestock!

GRAHAM, *stepping forward*:

> Permit us, Mauler, to give a brief account
> Of the seven-hour battle which began this morning and ended
> By plunging us all into the abyss.

MAULER:

Oh, everlasting slaughter! Nowadays
Things are no different from prehistoric times
When they bloodied each other's heads with iron bars!

GRAHAM:

Remember, Mauler, by our contract to deliver
Meat to you, you forced us to buy meat
In these of all times, and it had to be
From you, as only you had meat to sell.
Well, when you went away at noon, that Slift
Pulled the rope even tighter around our necks.
With harsh cries he kept on raising prices
Until they stood at ninety-five. But then
A halt was called by the ancient National Bank.
Bleating with responsibility, the old crone dumped
Canadian yearlings on the chaotic market, and prices stood
    quivering.
But Slift – that madman! – scarcely had he seen
The handful of widely-travelled steers but he grabbed them
    at ninety-five
As a drunkard who's already swilled an oceanful
And still feels thirsty greedily laps up one
Tiny drop more. The old crone shuddered at the sight.
But some people leaped to the beldame's side to hold her up –
Loew and Levi, Wallox and Brigham, the most reputable
    firms –
And offered all their possessions down to the last eraser
As pledges that they would bring forth the last remaining
    steer
From the Argentine and Canada within three days – they
    even promised
To get hold of unborn ones, ruthlessly
Anything that was steerlike, calfly, hoggish!
Slift yells: 'Three days? No! Today, today!'
And shoves the prices higher. And in floods of tears
The banks threw themselves into the death-struggle
Because they had to deliver the goods and therefore buy.

Sobbing, Levi himself punched one of Slift's brokers
In the belly, and Brigham tore his beard out
Screaming: Ninety-six! At that point
An elephant might have wandered in
And been crushed underfoot like a berry.
Even the pageboys, seized with despair, bit one another
Without saying a word, as horses in olden times
Would bite each other's flanks among their fighting riders!
Unsalaried clerks, famous for lack of interest in business
Were heard gnashing their teeth that day.
And still we bought and bought; we had to buy.
Then Slift said: One hundred! You could have heard a pin
      drop.
And as quietly as that the banks collapsed
Like trampled sponges – formerly strong and firm
Now suspending payment like respiration. Softly
Old Levi spoke, and all of us heard him: 'Now
Take over the packing plants yourselves, we can no longer
Fulfil our contracts', and so
Packer after packer, they sullenly laid
The shut-down, useless packing plants at your feet –
Yours and Slift's – and went away;
And the agents and salesmen snapped their brief-cases shut.
And at that moment, with a sigh as of liberation –
Since no more contracts compelled its purchase –
Livestock settled into the bottomless pit.
For unto prices it was given
To fall from quotation to quotation
As water hurtles from crag to crag
Deep down into the infinite. They didn't stop before thirty.
And so, Mauler, your contract became invalid.
Instead of gripping our throats you have strangled us.
What does it profit a man to grip the throat of a corpse?

MAULER:

So, Slift, that was how you managed the fight
I left on your hands!

SLIFT: Tear my head off.

MAULER:

What good is your head?
I'll take your hat, that's worth five cents!
What is to become
Of all that cattle no one has to buy?

THE STOCKBREEDERS:

Without becoming excited
We request you to tell us
Whether, when and with what
You wish to pay
For the bought but unpaid-for cattle.

MAULER:

At once. With this hat and this boot.
Here is my hat for ten million, here
My first shoe for five. I need the other.
Are you satisfied?

THE STOCKBREEDERS:

Alas, when moons ago
We led the frisky calf
And clean young steers
Carefully fattened, by ropes to the station in far-off Missouri
The family yelled after us
And even after the rolling trains
With voices broken by toil they yelled:
'Don't drink the money away, fellows, and
Let's hope prices will rise!'
What'll we do now? How
Can we go home? What
Shall we tell them
Showing the empty ropes
And empty pockets?
How can we go home in such a state, Mauler?

The man who was there before enters.

THE MAN: Is Mauler here? There's a letter from New York for
him.

MAULER: I *was* the Mauler to whom such letters were addressed.

He opens it and reads it aside: 'Recently, dear Pierpont, we wrote to tell you to buy meat. Today, however, we advise you to arrive at a settlement with the stockbreeders and limit the quantity of livestock, so as to give prices a chance to recover. To this end we shall gladly be of service to you. More tomorrow, dear Pierpont. – Your friends in New York.' No, no, that won't work.

GRAHAM: What won't work?

MAULER: I have friends in New York who claim to know a way out. It doesn't seem feasible to me. Judge for yourselves.

Gives them the letter.

How completely different
Everything seems now. Give up the chase, my friends.
Your property is gone: you must grasp that, it is lost.
But not because we are no longer blest with earthly
Goods – not everyone can be that –
Only because we have no feeling for higher things.
That's why we're poor!

MEYERS: Who are these friends of yours in New York?

MAULER: Horgan and Blackwell. Sell...

GRAHAM: Would that be Wall Street?

Whispering spreads throughout the gathering.

MAULER:
The inward man, so cruelly crushed within us...

THE PACKERS AND STOCKBREEDERS:
Noble Mauler, consent to bring yourself
To descend to us from your lofty
Meditations! Think of the chaos
That would swoop on everything, and take up –
Since you are needed, Mauler –
The burden of responsibility again!

MAULER:
I don't like to do it.
And I won't do it alone, for the grumbling in the stockyards
And the rat-tat-tat of machine guns

96

Still resound in my ears. It would only work
If it were sanctioned in a very grand style
And conceived as vital
To the public good.
Then it might work.

To Snyder:

Are there many Bible shops like this one?
SNYDER: Yes.
MAULER: How are they doing?
SNYDER: Badly.
MAULER:

Doing badly, but there are many of them.
If we promoted the cause of the Black Straw Hats
In a really big way – if you were equipped
With lots of soup and music
And suitable Bible quotations, even with shelter
In great emergencies – would you then speak
On our behalf, saying everywhere that we are good people?
Planning good things in bad times? For only
By taking extremest measures – measures that might seem
    harsh
Because they affect some people, quite a few really
In short: most people, nearly everybody –
Can we preserve this system now, the system
Of buying and selling which is here to stay
And also has its seamy side.

SNYDER: For nearly everybody. I understand. We would.
MAULER, *to the packers:*

I have merged your packing plants
As one ring and am taking over
Half of the stocks.

THE PACKERS: A great mind!
MAULER, *to the stockbreeders:*

My dear friends, listen!

They whisper.

The difficulty which oppressed us is lifting.
Misery, hunger, excesses, violence
Have one cause only and the cause is clear:
There was too much meat. The meat market was
All stuffed up this year and so the price of livestock
Sank to nothing. Now, to maintain it
We, packers and stockbreeders, have formed a united front
To set some limits to this unbridled breeding:
To restrict the livestock coming into market
And eliminate excess from the current supply. This means
Burning one-third of the livestock total.

ALL: Simple solution!

SNYDER, *saluting*:

    Might it not be possible – if all that cattle
Is so worthless that it can be burned –
Just to give it to the many standing out there
Who could make such good use of it?

MAULER, *smiling*:

    My dear Snyder, you have not grasped
The root of the situation. The many
Standing out there – *they are the buyers!*

To the others:

    It's hardly credible.

All smile for a long time.

    They may seem low, superfluous
Indeed, burdensome sometimes, but it cannot elude
Profounder insight that *they* are the buyers!
Likewise – there are very many who do not understand this –
    it is essential
To lock out a third of the workers.
It is also work that has clogged our markets and therefore
It must be limited.

ALL: The only way out!

MAULER: And wages lowered!

ALL: Columbus' egg!

MAULER:

All this is being done so that
In gloomy times of bloody confusion
Dehumanized humanity
When there is no end to the unrest in our cities
(For Chicago is again upset by talk of a general strike)
The brute strength of the short-sighted people
May not shatter its own tools and trample its own bread-
baskets underfoot
But peace and order may return. That is why we are willing
To facilitate by generous contributions
The work by which you Black Straw Hats encourage order.
It's true that there ought to be people among you again
Like that girl Joan, who inspires confidence
By her mere appearance.

A BROKER, *rushing in*: Glad tidings! The threatened strike has been suppressed. They've jailed the criminals who impiously troubled peace and order.

SLIFT:

Breathe freely now! The market's getting well!
Again the doldrums have been overcome.
The difficult task has once again been done
And once again a plan is finely spun
And the world resumes the way we like it run.

Organ.

MAULER:

And now, open wide your gates
Unto the weary and heavy laden and fill the pot with soup.
Tune up some music and we will sit
Upon your benches, in the very front row
To be converted.

SNYDER: Open the doors!

The doors are flung wide open.

THE BLACK STRAW HATS, *singing, eyes on the door*:
    Spread the net far out: they're bound to come!
    They've just abandoned the last redoubt!
    God's driving cold on them!
    God's driving rain on them!
    So they're bound to come! Spread the net far out!
    Welcome! Welcome! Welcome!
    Welcome to our humble home!

    Bolt everything tight so that none will escape!
    They're on their way down to us all right!
    If they've no work to do
    If they're deaf and blind too
    Not one will escape! So bolt everything tight!
    Welcome! Welcome! Welcome!
    Welcome to our humble home!

    Whatever may come, gather everything in!
    Hat and head and shoe and leg and scamp and scum!
    Its hat has gone sky-high
    So it comes right in to cry!
    Gather everything in, whatever may come!
    Welcome! Welcome! Welcome!
    Welcome to our humble home!

    Here we stand! Watch them coming down!
    Watch their misery drive them like animals to our hand!
    Look, they're bound to come down!
    Look, they're coming down!
    They can't get away from this spot: here we stand!
    Welcome! Welcome! Welcome!
    Welcome to our humble home!

Stockyards. Environs of Graham's Warehouse

The yards are almost empty. Only a few groups of workers are still passing by.

JOAN, *coming up to ask*: Did three men go by here asking for a letter?

Shouting from rear, spreading towards front. Then enter five men escorted by soldiers: the two from the union local and the three from the power stations. Suddenly one of the union men stands still and speaks to the soldiers.

THE MAN: If you're taking us to jail now, there's something you ought to know. We did what we did because we are for you.

A SOLDIER: Keep moving, if you're for us.

THE MAN: Wait a little!

THE SOLDIER: Getting scared, eh?

THE MAN: Yes, that too, but that's not what I'm talking about. I just want you to stand still a little so I can tell you why you have arrested us, because you don't know.

THE SOLDIERS, *laughing*: O.K., tell us why we arrested you.

THE MAN: Without property yourselves, you help men of property because you don't yet see any possibility of helping men without property.

THE SOLDIER: That's fine. Now let's move on.

THE MAN: Wait, I haven't finished the sentence: on the other hand, the working people in this town are starting to help the people without work. So the possibility is coming nearer. Now worry about that.

THE SOLDIER: I guess you want us to let you go, eh?

THE MAN: Didn't you understand me? We just want you to know that your time's coming soon too.

THE SOLDIERS: Can we go on now?

THE MAN: Yes, we can go on now.

They move on.

Joan stays where she is, watching the arrested men go. Then she hears two people talking beside her.

FIRST MAN: Who are those people?

SECOND MAN:

> Not one of them
> Cared only for himself.
> They ran without rest
> To get bread for strangers.

FIRST MAN: Why without rest?

SECOND MAN:

> The unjust man may cross the street in the open,
> But the just man hides.

FIRST MAN: What's being done to them?

SECOND MAN:

> Although they work for low wages and are useful to many men
> Not one of them lives out the years of his life
> Eats his bread, dies contented
> And is honourably buried, but
> They end before their time
> Struck down and trampled on and heaped with shame.

FIRST MAN: Why don't we ever hear about them?

SECOND MAN: If you read in the papers that certain criminals have been shot or thrown into prison, they're the ones.

FIRST MAN: Will it always be like that?

SECOND MAN: No.

As Joan turns to go, she is accosted by the reporters.

THE REPORTERS: Isn't this Our Lady of the Stockyards? Hi there! Things have gone wrong! The general strike was a flop. The stockyards are opening up again, but only for two-thirds of the personnel and only at two-thirds' pay. But meat prices are going up.

JOAN: Have the workers accepted this?

THE REPORTERS: Sure. Only a part of them knew the strike was being planned, and the cops drove that part out of the yards by force.

Joan falls to the ground.

b

In front of the Graham Company Storehouse

A group of workers with lanterns.

THE WORKERS: She must be lying here. She came from over there, and this is where she called out to our people that the city utilities planned to strike. The blizzard must have kept her from noticing the soldiers. One of them knocked her down with his rifle butt. I saw her distinctly for a moment. There she is! There should be more like her. No, that's not her! She was an old working woman. That girl isn't one of us. Let her lie there till the soldiers come; they'll pick her up.

12

DEATH AND CANONIZATION OF ST. JOAN
OF THE STOCKYARDS

The Black Straw Hats' House is now richly furnished and decorated. Its doors are flung wide open; the Black Straw Hats with new flags, the slaughterers, the stockbreeders and the wholesalers stand arranged in groups.

SNYDER:
Thus our task meets happy ending:
God's foothold has been found again.
For the highest good contending
We have faced the depths of pain.

Both our mounting and descending
Show what we can mean to you:
Lo, at last the happy ending!
Look, at last we've put it through!

Enter a group of poor people, with Joan at their head, supported by two policemen.

THE POLICEMEN: Here's a homeless woman we picked up in the stockyards in a sick condition. Her last permanent residence was here, she says.

Joan holds her letter high as though still anxious to deliver it.

JOAN:
The man who has perished will never
Take my letter from me.
Small enough service to a good cause, the only service
Demanded of me my whole life long! –
And I did not perform it.

While the poor people sit down on the benches to get their soup, Slift consults with the packers and Snyder.

SLIFT: It's our own Joan. Why, her coming is like an answer to our prayers. Let's cover her with glory; by her philanthropic work in the stockyards, her championship of the poor, and even her speeches against us, she helped us over some really difficult weeks. She shall be our St. Joan of the Stockyards! We will cultivate her as a saint and refuse her no jot of respect. The fact that she is shown under our auspices will prove that we hold humaneness in high regard.

MAULER:
May the pure and childlike soul
Ever figure on our roll;
May our humble choir delight
In her singing clear and glad;
May she damn whatever's bad
And defend our every right.

SNYDER:
Rise, Joan of the stockyards
Champion of the poor
Comforter of the lowest depths!

JOAN:
What a wind in the depths! What is that shrieking

The snow is trying to hush?
Eat your soup, you!
Don't spill your last bit of warmth, you
Ragamuffins! If only I had lived
As tranquilly as a cow
And yet delivered the letter that was entrusted to me!

THE BLACK STRAW HATS, *going up to her*:

Sudden daylight makes her ache
After nights of stupefaction!
Only human was your action!
Only human your mistake!

JOAN, *while the girls dress her in the Black Straw Hat uniform
        again*:

The noise of transport is starting again, you can hear it.
Another chance to stop it – wasted.
Again the world runs
Its ancient course unaltered.
When it was possible to change it
I did not come; when it was necessary
That I, little person, should help
I stayed on the sidelines.

MAULER:

Alas, that man cannot abide
In his distress the earthly bond
But with swift and haughty stride
Rushes past the everyday
Which he thinks will turn him gray
Past his target and beyond
Into worlds outside his ken
Endless worlds too high for men.

JOAN:

I spoke in every market place
And my dreams were numberless but
I did harm to the injured
And was useful to those who harmed them.

THE BLACK STRAW HATS:

Alas! All effort, sages write

Achieves but patchwork void of soul
If matter make not spirit whole.

THE PACKERS:

And ever 'tis a glorious sight
When soul and business unite!

JOAN:

One thing I have learned and I know it in your stead
Dying myself:
How can I say it – there's something inside you
And it won't come out! *What* do you know in your wisdom
That has no consequences?
I, for instance, did nothing.
Oh, let nothing be counted good, however helpful it may
    seem
And nothing considered honourable except that
Which will change this world once for all: that's what it needs.
Like an answer to their prayers I came to the oppressors!
Oh, goodness without consequences! Intentions in the dark!
I have changed nothing.
Swiftly vanishing without fear from this world
I say to you:
Take care that when you leave the world
You were not only good but are leaving
A good world!

GRAHAM: We'll have to see to it that her speeches only get
    through if they are reasonable. We mustn't forget that she
    has been in the stockyards.

JOAN:

For there is a gulf between top and bottom, wider
Than between Mount Himalaya and the sea
And what goes on above
Is not found out below
Or what happens below, above
And there are two languages, above and below
And two standards for measuring
And that which wears a human face
No longer knows itself.

THE PACKERS AND STOCKBREEDERS, *very loud, so as to shout
    Joan down*:
    Top and bottom must apply
    For the building to be high
    That's why everyone must stay
    In the place where they belong
    Day after day
    Man must do what suits his stature
    For if he forgets his nature
    All our harmonies go wrong.
    Underdogs have weight below
    The right man's right when up you go.
    Woe to him who'd rouse that host –
    Indispensable but
    Demanding, not
    To be done without
    And aware of that –
    Elements of the nethermost!

JOAN:
    But those who are down below are kept below
    So that the ones above may stay up there
    And the lowness of those above is measureless
    And even if they improve that would be
    No help, because the system they have made
    Is unique; exploitation
    And disorder, bestial and therefore
    Incomprehensible.

THE BLACK STRAW HATS, *to Joan*: Be a good girl! Hold your
    tongue!

THE PACKERS:
    Those who float in boundless spaces
    Cannot rise to higher places
    For to climb you need a rung
    And to reach for things aloft
    You must make a downward tread!

MAULER:
    Action, alas, may break a head!

THE BLACK STRAW HATS:

> Though your shoe is stained with gore

THE PACKERS:

> Do not try to pull it off!
> You will need it more and more.

THE BLACK STRAW HATS:

> Keep conduct high and spirit young.
> But do not forget to rue it!

THE PACKERS:

> Do anything!

THE BLACK STRAW HATS:

> But always do it
> With a twinge of conscience, for –
> Being given to contemplation
> And to self-vituperation –
> Your conscience will be sore!
> Men of trade, be informed:
> You cannot afford
> To forget the splendid
> Quite indispensable
> Word of the Lord
> Which is never ended
> And ever transformed!

JOAN:

> Therefore, anyone down here who says there is a God
> When none can be seen
> A God who can be invisible and yet help them
> Should have his head knocked on the pavement
> Until he croaks.

SLIFT: Listen, people, you've got to say something to shut that girl up. You must speak – anything you like, but loud!

SNYDER: Joan Dark, twenty-five years old, stricken by pneumonia in the stockyards of Chicago, in the service of God: a fighter and a sacrifice!

JOAN:

> And the ones that tell them they may be raised in spirit
> And still be stuck in the mud, they should have their heads

Knocked on the pavement. No!
Only force helps where force rules
And only men help where men are.

All sing the first verse of the chorale in order to stop Joan's speeches from being heard.

ALL:

Fill the full man's plate! Hosanna!
Greatness to the great! Hosanna!
To him that hath shall be given! Hosanna!
Give him city and state! Hosanna!
To the victor a sign from Heaven! Hosanna!

During these declamations loudspeakers begin to announce terrible news:

POUND CRASHES! BANK OF ENGLAND CLOSES FOR FIRST TIME IN 300 YEARS! EIGHT MILLION UNEMPLOYED IN U.S.A.! FIVE YEAR PLAN A SUCCESS! BRAZIL POURS A YEAR'S COFFEE HARVEST INTO OCEAN! SIX MILLION UNEMPLOYED IN GERMANY! THREE THOUSAND BANKS COLLAPSE IN U.S.A.! EXCHANGES AND BANKS CLOSED DOWN BY GOVERNMENT IN GERMANY! BATTLE BETWEEN POLICE AND UNEMPLOYED OUTSIDE FORD FACTORY IN DETROIT! MATCH TRUST, BIGGEST IN EUROPE, CRASHES! FIVE-YEAR PLAN IN FOUR YEARS!

Under the impression of this news those not engaged in declamation scream abuse at one another, as: 'You slaughtered too much livestock, you rotten butchers!' 'You should have raised more stock, you lousy stockbreeders!' 'You crazy money-grubbers, you should have employed more labour and handed out more pay-cheques! Who else will eat our meat?' 'It's the middleman that makes meat expensive!' 'It's the grain racket that raises livestock prices!' 'The railroads' freight rates are strangling us!' 'The banks' interest rates are ruining us!' 'Who can pay those rents for stables and silos?' 'Why don't you start ploughing under?' 'We did, but you aren't!' 'The guilt is yours and yours alone!' 'Things won't improve until you're hanged!' 'You should have been in jail years ago!' 'How come you're still at large?'

ALL *sing second and third verses of chorale. Joan is now inaudible.*

Pity the well-to-do! Hosanna!
Set them in Thy path! Hosanna!
Vouchsafe Thy grace, Hosanna!
And Thy help to him that hath! Hosanna!
Have mercy on the few! Hosanna!

Joan's talk is noticeably stopping.

ALL:

Aid Thy class, which in turn aids Thee, Hosanna!
With generous hand! Hosanna!
Stamp out hatred now! Hosanna!
Laugh with the laugher, allow, Hosanna!
His misdeeds a happy end! Hosanna!

During this verse the girls have been trying to pour some soup down Joan's throat. Twice she has pushed the plate back; the third time she seizes it, holds it high and then tips the contents out. Then she collapses and is now lying in the girls' arms, mortally stricken, with no sign of life. Snyder and Mauler step towards her.

MAULER: Give her the flag!

The flag is presented to her. It drops from her hands.

SNYDER: Joan Dark, twenty-five years of age, dead of pneumonia in the stockyards in the service of God, a fighter and a sacrifice!

MAULER:

Something pure
Without a flaw
Uncorrupted, helpful, whole –
It thrills us common folk to awe!
Rouses in our breast a newer
Better soul!

All stand in speechless emotion for a long time. At a sign from Snyder, all the flags are gently lowered over Joan until she is entirely covered by them. A rosy glow illumines the picture.

THE PACKERS AND STOCKBREEDERS:

> The boast of man is that he owns
> Immemorial desires
> By which towards the higher zones
> His spirit constantly aspires.
> He sees the stars upon their thrones
> Senses a thousand ways to heaven
> Yet downward by the flesh is driven;
> Then in shame his pride expires.

MAULER:

> A twofold something cuts and tears
> My sorely troubled inward state
> Like a jagged, deep-thrust knife:
> I'm drawn to what is truly great
> Free from self and the profit rate
> And yet impelled to business life
> All unawares!

ALL:

> Humanity! Two souls abide
> Within thy breast!
> Do not set either one aside:
> To live with both is best!
> Be torn apart with constant care!
> Be two in one! Be here, be there!
> Hold the low one, hold the high one –
> Hold the straight one, hold the sly one –
> Hold the pair!

NOTES ON 'ST. JOAN OF THE STOCKYARDS'

(The page numbers given in the Notes refer to an earlier edition of the play. Please subtract 88 to obtain the correct page numbers for this volume.)

In order to clarify the sequence of business transactions, newsboys may be sent across the stage or through the audience calling out:

page 93, preceding Scene 2
    'Meat kings in bloody duel!'
    'Meat prices are flattened!'
    'War between meat giants Mauler and Lennox!'
    'Mauler offers a pound of meat for a nickel!'
    'Lennox makes it four cents! Lennox warned by banks! How long can Lennox keep going? Mauler or Lennox - who will win?'

page 101, following Workers 2
    'Disaster faces stockyard workers!'
    'Now that Lennox has closed down, Mauler closes down! Half the workers in Chicago stockyards out of work! Winter at the gates!'

page 131, preceding Scene 6
    'Pierpont Mauler goes among the speculators!'
    'He contracts to take the slaughterers' products off their hands!'
    'The stockbreeders' situation is uncertain, because the slaughterhouses still aren't buying livestock. They still think the price of livestock will go down!'

page 138, preceding Scene 7
    'Strange goings-on in the livestock market!'
    'Secret purchases of livestock in Illinois and Arkansas!'
    'Livestock prices rising! Unrest grows among stockyards workers, in fifth week of lockout!'
    'Packing plants plan support measures! Feverish activity among charity committees!'

page 146, preceding Scene 8
    'No work in stockyards yet!'
    'Misery grows among masses! Small businessmen no longer able to pay store rent! Who is buying up livestock on the sly? Interview with Pierpont Mauler! Pierpont Mauler doesn't know identity of mysterious cornerer!'
    'First snowfall! Snow blankets Chicago!'

page 152, preceding Scene 9
    'Uproar on livestock exchange! Tremendous rise in livestock prices!'
    'A Black Straw Hat girl, Joan Dark, says she won't leave the stockyards before work starts again!'
    'Tens of thousands wait in the yards, in spite of snow and cold!'

page 154, following Mauler 1
    'Tariff barriers fall in South! Sudden large demand for export livestock!'
    'Tariff barriers fall! Entirely unexpected!'

page 154, preceding Mauler 2
    'Southern tariff barriers down! Demand for export livestock! Where has livestock gone? Not a head of cattle to be found in Illinois or Arkansas!'